TO

_____

FROM

_____

DATE

_____

# CATHOLIC CHILDREN'S
# BIBLE

*Edited by*
Bart Tesoriero

*Nihil Obstat*
Right Reverend Archimandrite Francis Vivona,
S.T.M., J.C.L.

*Imprimatur*
Most Reverend Joseph A. Pepe, D.D., J.C.D.

*Date*
March 25, 2015
*The Annunciation of the Lord*

LCCN: 2014957954
ISBN 978-1-61796-156-4
Text © 2015 Aquinas Kids, Phoenix, Arizona
Printed in China

# *Table of Contents*
## OLD TESTAMENT

# Table of Contents

# Table of Contents

# Table of Contents

# THE OLD TESTAMENT
## God Creates the Heavens and the Earth

In the beginning, a long, long, time ago, before the world was made, even before there was the sky, or the sun, or the moon, or the stars, there was God.

God is like a family: the Father, the Son, and the Holy Spirit. God was completely happy, yet He wanted to share His happiness with others. God wanted a family, with whom He could share His love. He decided to create people!

First of all, God made a place where men, women, and children could live. He said, "Let there be light," and there was light! Then God created the heavens, the sky. He gathered the waters of the earth together into oceans, seas, rivers, and lakes. He made the trees and plants. God created the sun to rule over the day and the moon to rule over the night. He made the stars. Then He created the fish and the birds, followed by all the animals and creatures of the earth. God looked at all He had made, and He said, "It is good!"

However, God was not finished with His creation. In fact, He had saved the very best part for last.

# Adam and Eve

On the final day of His creation, God created Adam and Eve. God formed man out of the clay of the ground and blew into his nostrils the breath of life, and man became a living being. God said, "It is not good for the man to be alone. I will make a suitable partner for him." So the Lord cast a deep sleep on the man. He took out one of his ribs and closed up its place with flesh. God then built up into a woman the rib taken from the man. God made man and woman in His image and likeness.

God placed Adam and Eve in a beautiful garden paradise. He told them to cultivate the Garden and to care for it. Sweet-smelling flowers and luscious fruits grew everywhere. Lively birds chirped and the animals played together.

God told Adam and Eve that they could eat of the fruit of every tree in the Garden except for the tree of the knowledge of good and evil. He told them that if they ate of it, they would die. When God finished creating Adam and Eve, He said, "Now that is very good!" God made everything in six days. God rested from His work on the seventh day and He blessed the day. That day is called the Sabbath.

# The Fall of Adam and Eve

Before creating the world, God had created angels. Angels are pure spirits that serve as God's messengers, who worship Him at all times. One of them, Lucifer, rebelled against God, and some of the angels joined him. Saint Michael the Archangel fought against Lucifer and threw him out of heaven, down to the earth. Lucifer's name was changed to Satan, which means the adversary, or the accuser.

One day Satan, the devil, came as a serpent to tempt Eve. He told her that if she ate of the forbidden fruit, she would become like God. Eve saw that the fruit looked appetizing, and she decided to eat it. She then gave it to Adam, who also ate it. When they ate the forbidden fruit, they realized they had displeased God by disobeying Him.

Almighty God was very unhappy with Adam and Eve. They had lost His presence in their hearts, and could not remain in the Garden. God told the serpent that he would have to crawl around on his belly and be apart from all the other animals and wild creatures. But God also promised to send a Redeemer to save all people, a Redeemer who would be born of a woman. The Redeemer would crush the head of the serpent, and the serpent would strike at His heel.

# Noah and the Ark

Eve bore Adam two sons, Cain and Abel. One day Cain offered to God some fruits of his field, while Abel offered to the Lord the very best of his flock. The Lord favored Abel, but He was not pleased with Cain's second-best offering. Cain grew angry with Abel and killed him. The Lord said, "The blood of your brother cries out to me!" The Lord cursed Cain because he had killed Abel. Cain then became a restless wanderer over the earth.

Adam and Eve had more children, who spread out over the face of the earth. People forgot about God. They sinned and became wicked. God told a good man named Noah that He had decided to put an end to everyone living on the earth. He told Noah to build a large boat called an ark, as He was going to send a flood upon the earth. God told Noah to go into the ark with his wife, his family, and pairs of each kind of animal, one male and one female.

God sent a great flood upon the earth. It rained for forty days and forty nights. After the flood, Noah built an altar and offered a sacrifice to God to thank Him for His goodness. God put a rainbow in the sky as a sign that He would never again destroy the earth with a flood.

# The Tower of Babel

Noah's sons were named Shem, Ham, and Japheth. They also had children, and in time the world was again filled with many people. In fact, the whole world spoke the same language, using the same words! One day, in a place called Shinar, the people decided to build a tower up to the heavens, to make a name for themselves in the whole earth.

God saw what they were doing, and said, "If now, while they are one people, all speaking the same language, these inhabitants have begun to do this, nothing will later stop them from doing whatever they want to do. Let us then go down and there confuse their language, so that one will not understand what another says."

The Lord then confused their speech, so that the people could not finish building the tower, because they did not understand each other. That is why the tower was called the Tower of Babel, because there the Lord confused the speech of the whole world. It was from there that He scattered the people all over the face of the earth.

# God Calls Abram

Shem, the son of Noah, had many descendants over the centuries. One of these was a man named Terah, who lived in a place called Ur, near modern-day Iraq. Terah had three sons, one of whom was named Abram. Abram's wife was Sarai. She was barren, which means she was unable to have any children. Terah took Abram and Sarai, and Abram's nephew Lot, and brought them out of Ur to a place called Haran, where they settled.

One day, God called Abram and said to him, "Go forth from the land of your kinsfolk and from your father's house to a land that I will show you. I will make of you a great nation, and I will bless you. I will make your name great, so that you will be a blessing. I will bless those who bless you and curse those who curse you. All the families of the earth shall find blessing in you."

Abram took his wife Sarai and his nephew Lot, and they set out for the land of Canaan. Abram passed through the land as far as the sacred place at Shechem. The Lord appeared to Abram and said, "To your descendants I will give this land." Then Abram built an altar there to the Lord.

# Sodom and Gomorrah

Abram and Lot settled in the land of Canaan. Abram said to Lot, "Let there be no strife between you and me, or between your herdsmen and mine. Please separate from me. If you prefer the left, I will go to the right; if you prefer the right, I will go to the left." Lot chose the whole Jordan Plain, and pitched his tents near Sodom, which was a wicked city.

The Lord appeared to Abram and said: "Between you and me I will establish my covenant, and multiply you exceedingly. No longer shall you be called Abram; your name shall be Abraham, for I am making you the father of many nations." God also promised to give Abraham a son.

Later, the Lord told Abraham that the outcry against Sodom and Gomorrah was so great that He had to act. He agreed to be merciful if even ten just people were found in the city. However, it was not so. God's angels urged Lot and his family to leave Sodom. When Lot hesitated, the angels seized him and his family and led them to safety. They said, "Flee for your life! Do not look back or stop." God rained down fire upon the land, and He destroyed the cities of Sodom and Gomorrah. But Lot's wife looked back, and she was turned into a pillar of salt.

# Abraham and Isaac

God had promised to give Abraham and Sarah a son. In her old age, Sarah bore Abraham a son, whom they named Isaac, which means "laughter." Some years later, God put Abraham to the test. "Abraham!" He said, "Take your son Isaac, whom you love, and go to the land of Moriah. There you shall offer him up as a sacrifice on a mount that I will point out to you." Early the next day Abraham saddled his donkey, took his son Isaac, two servants, and the wood for the sacrifice, and set out for the mountain of Moriah.

When they drew near, Abraham told his servants, "Stay here, while the boy and I go on further. We will worship and then come back to you." Abraham laid the wood on Isaac's shoulders, while he himself carried the fire and the knife. Isaac asked, "Where is the sheep for the holocaust?" Abraham answered, "God Himself will provide the lamb."

Abraham built an altar, arranged the wood, and tied up his son Isaac. Then Abraham lifted the knife to slaughter his son, but God sent an angel to stop him. God told Abraham, "Because you did not hold back from Me your beloved son, I will bless you abundantly and give you more descendants than the stars of heaven."

# Jacob and Esau

Abraham died as a friend of God. Isaac married Rebecca, who gave birth to twins, Esau, her firstborn, and Jacob. Esau grew up to be a hunter. Jacob preferred living in tents. One day Esau traded his birthright as firstborn son to Jacob in return for a bowl of stew. Rebecca tricked Isaac into thinking that Jacob was Esau, and with a special blessing, Isaac made Jacob his heir. Esau was very angry, so Jacob went to live with his uncle Laban in Haran.

That night, after a weary day of travel, Jacob dreamed of a ladder from earth to heaven, with the angels of God going up and down its steps. The Lord stood beside Jacob and promised to fulfill all His promises to Abraham and Isaac. Jacob set up a memorial stone at that place and called it Bethel, which means "the house of God."

Jacob journeyed on to Haran, where he lived with his uncle, working many years to marry Rachel and Leah, the daughters of Laban. Laban's sons began to resent Jacob, for God was blessing him with flocks and herds, so Jacob left to return home, with his wives, his 12 sons, and one daughter.

# The Reunion

As he neared his homeland, Jacob sent messengers ahead. They reported that his brother Esau was coming to meet him with an army. Jacob divided his family and herds into two camps. "If Esau should attack and overwhelm one camp," he thought, "the other camp may still survive." He prayed fervently, reminding God of His promises to him and his descendants, and asked God to save him from Esau.

Jacob selected hundreds of goats, sheep, camels, cows, bulls, and donkeys, and sent them as gifts to Esau. At night Jacob was alone, when suddenly a man appeared who wrestled with him until dawn. When the man realized he could not win, he struck Jacob's hip at the socket, wrenching it out of place. Jacob would not let him go until he blessed him. The man said, "You shall no longer be spoken of as Jacob, but as Israel, because you have contended with divine and human beings and have prevailed." Jacob then realized that he had wrestled with a messenger from God.

That day Jacob went to meet Esau, followed by his wives and children. Esau embraced him and kissed him as he wept. Then they parted as brothers reunited in the Lord.

# Joseph and the Coat of Many Colors

Jacob had twelve sons, including Joseph, who was born when Jacob was old. Jacob loved Joseph the most of all his sons. He made him a beautiful coat of many colors. Joseph's brothers became jealous when they saw this and they would not even greet him.

One night, Joseph dreamed that he was with his brothers, tying up sheaves, or bunches, of grain in the field. The next day, he told his brothers about the dream, how his sheaf rose to an upright position, and their sheaves formed a ring around his and bowed down to it. "Are you really going to make yourself king over us?" his brothers asked him. "Are you going to rule over us?" They hated Joseph even more because of his talk about his dreams.

Then Joseph had a new dream, which he again shared with his family. "I had another dream, Joseph said, and this time, the sun, moon, and eleven stars bowed down to me." Jacob said to his son, "Can it be that I and your mother and your brothers are going to bow to the ground before you?" Joseph's brothers were very angry at him, but his father reflected about the matter.

# Joseph Is Sold into Slavery

One day, all the sons of Jacob except Joseph went to pasture their father's flocks at Shechem. Jacob sent Joseph out to visit his brothers. They saw him coming from a distance, and they cried, "Here comes that master dreamer! Come on, let us kill him and say that a wild beast devoured him. We shall then see what comes of his dreams."

But Joseph's brother Reuben said, "Instead of shedding blood, let us throw him into a cistern here in the desert." He hoped to rescue Joseph and return him to Jacob. So they took Joseph, stripped him, and threw him into the cistern.

A caravan of traders on their way to Egypt passed by, and the brothers decided to sell Joseph to them for twenty pieces of silver. They killed a goat, dipped his coat in its blood, and had the coat taken to Jacob, who thought that a wild beast had eaten his son. He was stricken with grief, and mourned.

The traders sold Joseph to a man who served the Pharaoh, or ruler, of Egypt. The man's wife tried to get Joseph to sin. He refused and she had him thrown into jail. After a long time, Joseph was released and ended up serving the Pharaoh as the governor of Egypt.

# Joseph Saves His People

God had revealed to Joseph through a dream of the Pharaoh that there would be seven years of plenty and seven years of famine in the land. Therefore Joseph had the people store up grain so they would have food to eat.

When the famine came, Jacob sent his sons to Egypt to buy grain. Joseph recognized his brothers, but they did not recognize him. Joseph tested his brothers, to see if they had turned from their evil ways. He also wanted to see his father Jacob, and to meet his younger brother Benjamin, about whom he heard his brothers speak.

After testing his brothers for a season, Joseph revealed himself to them. "I am Joseph, your brother! How is my father Jacob?" Joseph wept loudly and embraced his brothers, gave them wonderful gifts, and sent them home to their father. When Jacob learned that his beloved son was still alive, he journeyed with his entire household to Egypt to see him. Joseph ran to embrace him, weeping. "Now I can die with joy," said Jacob, "because I have seen your face." Joseph gave land to his father and brothers, and the Hebrew people became a great nation in Egypt.

# The Birth of Moses

Many years passed. A new Pharaoh ruled Egypt. He feared that the Hebrews would become more powerful than his own people. He made them his slaves. He also commanded that every Hebrew baby boy be drowned in the Nile River.

A certain Hebrew woman gave birth to a little boy, whom she loved very much. She made a basket out of plant leaves and sorrowfully put the basket among the reeds near the river. Her daughter Miriam hid in the bushes to watch.

One day the daughter of the Pharaoh came down to the river to bathe. She was greatly surprised find a little baby boy floating in a basket! She decided to adopt him and raise him as her own son. She called his name Moses, which means 'saved out of the water.'

Moses grew up and saw how the Egyptians forced the Hebrews to work very hard. One day he saw an Egyptian strike a Hebrew. In his anger, Moses killed the Egyptian and hid his body in the sand. When Pharaoh heard what had happened, he sent soldiers to arrest Moses and put him to death. However, Moses fled hundreds of miles away to a land called Midian, in Arabia.

# The Burning Bush

Moses became a shepherd in Midian, and married a woman named Zipporah. One day, while he was tending his sheep, Moses came to Horeb, the mountain of God. Moses saw there a burning bush which was not consumed by the fire. As he approached the bush, God called out to him, "Moses, Moses!" Stunned, Moses answered, "Here I am."

God commanded Moses to remove his sandals, for he was standing on holy ground. He told him, "I am the God of your fathers, the God of Abraham, Isaac, and Jacob. I have seen the affliction of My people Israel. I have come down to rescue them from the Egyptians and lead them into a good and spacious land, a land flowing with milk and honey. I will send you to Pharaoh to lead My people out of Egypt."

Moses said, "Who am I that I should go to Pharaoh and lead the Israelites out of Egypt?" God answered, "I will be with you. When you bring My people out of Egypt, you will worship Me on this very mountain." "But what is Your name?" persisted Moses. God replied, "I am who I am. You shall tell the Israelites: I AM sent me to you." God also appointed Aaron, the brother of Moses, to help him.

# The Passover of the Lord

Moses told the Pharaoh, "Thus says the Lord: 'Let my people go, so they can worship Me.'" But Pharaoh refused, so God turned the waters of Egypt into blood. He caused frogs to cover the land. Pharaoh asked Moses to stop the plague, and he would free the Hebrews. However, Pharaoh did not keep his promise. The Lord sent plagues of gnats, flies, and disease, but Pharaoh would not let the Hebrews go. The Lord sent a plague of sores and boils, and then plagues of hail, locusts, and darkness upon Egypt.

Then Moses said, "Thus says the Lord: 'At midnight I will go forth through Egypt. Every first-born in this land shall die, of man and animals.'" The Lord told Moses to tell the people to procure a lamb, and to offer it during the evening twilight. They were to apply its blood it to their doorposts and lintels. They were to eat it with sandals on their feet and staffs in their hands. God said, "It is the Passover of the Lord. For on this same night I will go through Egypt, striking down every first-born of the land, and executing judgment on all the gods of Egypt. But the blood will mark your houses. Seeing the blood, I will pass over you."

# God Sets His People Free

CR ● ꝲꝲ

The Israelites did as the Lord had commanded Moses and
Aaron. At midnight the Lord slew every first-born in the
land of Egypt, from the first-born of Pharaoh to the first-born
of the prisoner in the cell, as well as the first-born of
the animals. Pharaoh and all the Egyptians arose in the
night, and there was loud weeping throughout Egypt.

Pharaoh summoned Moses and Aaron and said, "Leave my
people at once, you and the Israelites with you! Go and
worship the Lord as you said. Take your flocks, too, and
your herds, and be gone." However, he then chased the
Hebrews to the Red Sea. Moses told the people, "Be not
afraid! The Lord himself will fight for you!" Moses stretched
forth his staff, and God parted the waters of the Red Sea. The
Hebrews passed over on dry ground. The Egyptians followed
after them, right into the midst of the sea.

After the Israelites had crossed over safely, the Lord told
Moses to stretch out his hand over the sea, and the waters
flowed back, covering Pharaoh's chariots and charioteers.
When Israel saw the great power of God, they believed in
the Lord and in His servant, Moses.

# Manna in the Desert

Then Moses and the Israelites sang this song to the Lord: "I will sing unto the Lord, for He has triumphed gloriously; the horse and chariot cast into the sea! My strength and my courage is the Lord, and He has become my savior. He is my God, I praise Him; the God of my fathers, I extol Him."

Moses led the people out to the desert of Shur. They marched for three days without finding water. They arrived at Marah, where they could not drink the water, because it was too bitter. The Lord told Moses to throw a certain piece of wood into the water, and it became fresh.

Two months after they left Egypt, the people then came into the desert of Sin. Here in the desert they again cried out to Moses and Aaron, this time for food. In His mercy the Lord sent quail into their camp. He also sent a sweet bread called manna, which appeared like dew on the desert ground.

The Israelites gathered this manna in the morning, and it fed them all day long. They ate this manna for forty years, until they reached the land of Canaan. Thus God fed His people and gave them to drink in all the years of their wandering, to prove that He will always provide for us.

# The Ten Commandments

⎯⎯⎯⎯⎯⎯ ⌘ ⎯⎯⎯⎯⎯⎯

Three months after leaving Egypt, the Israelites came to Mount Sinai. God called Moses and his servant Joshua up to the mountain and told him to tell the people that if they remained faithful to the Lord, He would continue to protect them and would make them His own chosen people.

Then God delivered to Moses the Ten Commandments:

**"I am the Lord your God. You shall not have other gods besides Me.**
**You shall not take the name of the Lord, your God, in vain.**
**Remember to keep holy the Sabbath day.**
**Honor your father and your mother.**
**You shall not kill.**
**You shall not commit adultery.**
**You shall not steal.**
**You shall not bear false witness against your neighbor.**
**You shall not desire your neighbor's wife.**
**You shall not desire your neighbor's goods."**

When the Lord had finished speaking to Moses, He gave him the two stone tablets, on which He had written the Ten Commandments.

# The Golden Calf

⊂⊃ • ⊂⊃

Moses was on Mount Sinai with the Lord for forty days and forty nights. When the people realized he was delayed in returning to them, they went to Aaron. "Come," they said, "make us a god who will be our leader. As for the man, Moses, who brought us out of the land of Egypt, we do not know what has happened to him."

Aaron replied, "Have your wives and children take off their golden earrings and bring them to me." Aaron accepted their offering, and made a molten calf with a carving tool. Then the people cried out, "This is your God, O Israel, who brought you out of the land of Egypt!"

Aaron built an altar before the golden calf and proclaimed a feast of the Lord. The people offered sacrifices to the golden calf. Then they ate and got drunk, and rose up to have a wild party.

The Lord said to Moses, "Go down at once to your people, whom you brought out of the land of Egypt, for they have become depraved. They have turned aside from the way I pointed out to them, making for themselves a molten calf and worshiping it. Let my anger blaze up against them."

# Moses Breaks the Tablets

Moses implored God, "Why, O Lord, should your wrath blaze up against your own people, whom You brought out of the land of Egypt with such great power? Please relent in punishing your people." So the Lord relented in the punishment he had threatened to inflict on His people.

Moses then went down the mountain with the two tablets of the Ten Commandments in his hands. As he and Joshua drew near the camp, he saw the calf and the dancing. With that, Moses grew so angry that he threw the tablets down and broke them on the base of the mountain. He then threw the golden calf into the fire, ground it into powder, mixed it with water and made the Israelites drink it.

Then the Lord said to Moses, "Cut two stone tablets like the former." He continued, "Write down My words, for in agreement with them I have made a covenant with you and with Israel." So Moses stayed there with the Lord for forty days and forty nights, without eating any food or drinking any water, and he wrote on the tablets the words of the covenant between God and His chosen people. In obedience to God Moses wrote again the Ten Commandments.

# Worship in the Desert and the Death of Moses

――――――― ✆ • ✆ ―――――――

The Lord commanded Moses to build a Dwelling Place where the people could worship the Lord in the desert. He also commanded Moses to build the Ark of the Covenant, a sacred chest covered with gold. The Ark contained the two tablets of the Law, as well as some manna and the rod of Aaron. Moses took up a collection among the people and had their skilled workers construct the Tent of Meeting, the sacred Dwelling Place of the Lord in the desert.

The Lord commanded that the high priest Aaron and his sons wear special vestments in their ministry of worship before the Lord. Moses blessed the people and anointed the Dwelling and everything in it with oil. He also vested Aaron with the sacred vestments and anointed him and his sons as priests unto the Lord. Then a cloud covered the meeting tent, and the glory of the Lord filled the Dwelling.

Moses led the people for forty years in the desert. Then the Lord commanded Moses to go to Mount Nebo, and view the Promised Land, the land which He had sworn to give Abraham, Isaac and Jacob, and their descendants. Moses, the servant of God, died on Mount Nebo at the age of 120.

# Israel Enters the Promised Land

After Moses died, the Lord said to Joshua, son of Nun, "Be strong and courageous, for it is you who must bring the Israelites into the land which I promised them on oath. Do not fear nor be dismayed, for the Lord, your God, is with you wherever you go. Prepare to cross the Jordan with all the people into the land I will give the Israelites."

Joshua and the people crossed over into the land of Canaan. They needed to capture Jericho, a large city with strong walls. God commanded the people to march around Jericho for seven days, led by the priests who were to carry the Ark of the Covenant, with seven priests carrying ram's horns in front of the Ark.

For six days the priests sounded the horns, but the people remained silent. On the seventh day, Joshua told the people to march around the city seven times, and the seventh time to shout as the priests blew their horns. At the sound of the horns and the shouts of the people, the walls of Jericho came tumbling down, and the Israelites captured the city. In time, Israel took possession of the land which God had promised to Abraham and to his descendants forever.

# Joshua Calls Israel to Witness

———— ❧ • ❧ ————

Many years later, after the Lord had given the Israelites rest from all of their enemies, Joshua summoned all the people, with their leaders, to a place named Shechem.

"I am old and advanced in years," Joshua said. "You have seen all that the Lord your God has done for you against all the nations that were against you. It was He who brought your father Abraham from Ur and led him to the land of Canaan. God gave him Isaac, and to Isaac He gave Jacob and Esau. God sent Moses and Aaron, and through them He led you out of Egypt through the Red Sea. It was not your sword or bow that defeated all your enemies, but the Lord Himself. He has kept all His promises to you, and given you this land.

"Therefore," Joshua said, "fear the Lord and serve Him alone. If it does not please you to serve the Lord, decide today whom you will serve. As for me and my house, we will serve the Lord!" The people responded, "Far be it from us to forsake the Lord for other gods. We will also serve the Lord." Joshua made a covenant with the people. Then, after fulfilling all the commands of the Lord, Joshua died, and was buried in the land of Israel.

# Gideon

As time passed, the Israelites began to forsake the Lord and worship other gods. The Lord would then give them over to the power of their enemies. Israel would cry out to the Lord, and He would raise up a deliverer, called a judge, for them.

The Israelites offended the Lord, and so He delivered them into the power of the people of Midian. Every year the Midianites destroyed the produce of all the land of Israel, so that there was no food for the people or their livestock. The Hebrews cried out to God for help.

The Lord sent an angel to a man of Israel named Gideon. He said to Gideon, "The Lord is with you, O champion!" The angel told Gideon to fight against Midian, and the Lord would give him the victory. Gideon asked the Lord for signs, and the Lord gave them to him. Then Gideon gathered an army. The Lord told Gideon to reduce the size of his army to just 300 men. Gideon gave his men horns and empty jars with torches inside them. The warriors came to the camp of the Midians, blew their horns, and broke their jars. They cried out, "A sword for the Lord and Gideon!" The Midianites were confused and killed one another, and the Lord delivered His people Israel.

# Ruth and Naomi

Many years later, a famine struck the land of Israel. A man of Bethlehem named Elimelech departed from there with his wife Naomi and his two sons, and went to the land of Moab. He died, and his sons married two Moabite women, named Orpah and Ruth.

After some time, both sons died, and Naomi decided to return to Bethlehem. She told Orpah and Ruth to go back to their mother's home, and to find husbands in Moab. Orpah kissed Naomi goodbye, but Ruth stayed with her. "Do not ask me to abandon you," Ruth said. "Wherever you go, I will go; wherever you live, I will live. Your people shall be my people, and your God shall be my God."

They journeyed to Bethlehem at the beginning of the barley harvest. Naomi had a well-known relative named Boaz, who owned a large barley field. Ruth went to gather leftover ears of grain from his field, and he noticed her. When Boaz heard Ruth's story, and how she had stayed with Naomi, he was kind to her. Naomi told Ruth to sleep at his feet on the threshing floor. Boaz awoke and took Ruth as his wife. Ruth became the mother of Obed, who became the father of Jesse, who became the father of King David.

# Samuel Hears the Voice of God

———— ⊂⨀⨾ • ⨾⨀⊃ ————

Some time after these events, a woman named Hannah
begged God to give her a son, for she was childless. God
heard her prayer and she bore a son whom she named
Samuel, which means 'God has heard.'

Hannah took Samuel, at three years of age, to the temple
and consecrated him to the Lord. One night, the Lord
called Samuel three times, and Samuel finally understood
that God was calling him to be His prophet. When Samuel
grew up, he helped the people listen to and obey God.

The Israelites wanted a king, and Samuel explained that
God was their king. However, the people kept begging for a king
like all the other nations, and so God told Samuel to anoint Saul
as the king of Israel.

The Lord sent Saul on a mission against the enemies of
Israel. However, Saul disobeyed the Lord and did not
complete the task God had given him. Samuel told Saul that
God was displeased with him. Samuel did not see Saul
again, until the day of his death. Still, Samuel grieved for
Saul, and the Lord regretted that He had made Saul the
king of Israel.

# Samuel Anoints David as King

The Lord said to Samuel: "Fill your horn with oil. I am sending you to Jesse of Bethlehem, for from his sons I have chosen my king." Samuel replied: "How can I go? Saul will hear of it and kill me." The Lord answered: "Say, 'I have come to sacrifice to the Lord.' Invite Jesse to the sacrifice, and you are to anoint for me the one I point out to you."

Samuel did as the Lord had commanded him. He looked at Eliab, the oldest son of Jesse. He thought, "Surely this the one God has chosen." But the Lord said to Samuel: "Do not judge from his appearance or from his lofty stature, because I have rejected him. Not as man sees does God see, because man sees the appearance, but the Lord looks into the heart."

In the same way Jesse presented seven sons before Samuel, but Samuel said to Jesse, "The Lord has not chosen any one of these. Are these all the sons you have?" Jesse replied, "There is still the youngest, who is tending the sheep." Samuel said, "Send for him." Jesse had the young man brought to them. He was ruddy, and strong. The Lord said, "Anoint him, for this is he." Then Samuel anointed him in the midst of his brothers and from that day on, the spirit of the Lord rushed upon David.

# David and Goliath

A war broke out between the Israelites, who were led by King Saul, and the Philistines. A terrible giant named Goliath dared any Israelite to fight him hand to hand. The Israelites were so frightened that none of them had the courage to come out to fight Goliath. But David said, "I will fight this Philistine!"

David picked five smooth stones, took his sling, and went forth to meet the giant. Goliath laughed at David, but David said, "Today the Lord shall deliver you into my hand. I will strike you down and cut off your head. For the battle is the Lord's, and He shall deliver you into our hands." Then David whirled a stone in his sling and flung it at the giant. The stone hit Goliath so hard that he fell to the ground. David cut off his head, and the Israelites won a great victory.

King Saul put David in charge of his army. However, the king grew resentful of David because the people honored David more than himself. Saul then tried to kill David. David had to flee to the country, where men gathered about him who fought with him against the enemies of Israel. Meanwhile, Saul and his armies suffered a great defeat from the Philistines, and Saul died on the field of battle. David wept for Saul, for although Saul had fought against him, still David loved him and his sons.

# David Dances Before the Ark

After King Saul died, David was chosen as king of Israel. David was thirty years old. The Philistines, who were enemies of Israel, rose up against David, but the Lord gave him great victories over them.

The Philistines had captured the Ark of God in a battle with Saul, but God had punished them for taking the Ark. They then put the Ark on a cart drawn by oxen, which pulled the cart to a town of Judah. David therefore assembled 30,000 men of Israel and set out to return the Ark to its rightful place in Jerusalem, the City of David.

David had the priests of the Lord carry the Ark on their shoulders. He sacrificed an ox and a fatted calf to the Lord. Then David danced before the Lord with abandon, as he and all the Israelites brought up the Ark of the Lord with great shouts of joy and the blasts of the trumpet. The Ark was placed in the tent that David had set up for it. King David offered more sacrifices unto the Lord. He then blessed the people in the name of the Lord. Finally, King David gave each family a loaf of bread, a cut of roast meat, and a raisin cake. With this, all the people left for their homes.

# King David Prays for Forgiveness

When he was older, King David remained in Jerusalem while his soldiers went out to fight the enemies of Israel. One evening, from his roof, he saw a beautiful woman. She was Bathsheba, the wife of Uriah, one of his soldiers, who was out fighting with the rest of his army. David took Bathsheba and had relations with her. Bathsheba conceived a child from David.

David tried to hide the matter by calling her husband Uriah back from the war, but it did not work. So David told his general to put Uriah where he would be killed by the enemy. David then sent for Bathsheba and made her his wife. But the Lord was displeased with what David had done.

The Lord sent Nathan, a prophet, to confront David with his sin. David confessed his sin, and prayed that God would forgive him. Nathan answered David, "The Lord has forgiven your sin: you shall not die. But since you have utterly rejected the Lord by this deed, the child born to you must surely die."

The child died, and David mourned him. Then the Lord gave David and Bathsheba another son, whom they named Solomon.

# The Temple of Solomon
―――――― ❧ • ❧ ――――――

King David ruled for 40 years. At his death, he left a great
and united kingdom. Before he died, David chose his son
Solomon to succeed him as king of Israel. He directed
Solomon to build a great temple to the Lord, using the
plans, money, and supplies that David had stored up.

One night, the Lord appeared to Solomon in a dream, and
told him to ask for whatever he wanted. Solomon asked for
the wisdom to rule his people with justice and goodness.
The Lord was so pleased with Solomon's request that He
gave Solomon great wisdom. He also gave him riches,
honor, and long life.

Solomon and all the people of Israel built a grand and
beautiful temple for the Lord. At the dedication of the
temple, all the priests and leaders of Israel, as well as many
of the people, gathered in Jerusalem. The people brought
countless bulls and sheep to be offered to the Lord in
sacrifice on His holy altar. Everyone was very excited and
filled with praise in their hearts as Solomon took his place
before the altar and lifted his hands unto the Lord.

# Solomon Prays for Wisdom

Solomon stood at the altar of the Lord in the presence of the whole community of Israel, and stretched forth his hands toward heaven. He prayed, "Lord, God of Israel, there is no God like You in heaven above or on earth below. You keep Your covenant of kindness with Your servants who are faithful to You with their whole heart. You have kept the promise You made to my father David, Your servant. Look kindly on the prayer and petition of Your servant, O Lord, my God, and listen to the cry of supplication which I, Your servant, utter before You this day. May Your eyes watch night and day over this temple. Listen to the petitions of Your people Israel which they offer in this place. Listen from Your heavenly dwelling and grant pardon."

The Lord sent fire from heaven to consume the sacrifices of 22,000 oxen and 120,000 sheep, and the glory of the Lord filled the temple. All the Israelites fell down with their faces to the earth and adored, praising the Lord, "for he is good, for his mercy endures forever." The priests and Levites played on their musical instruments. Across from them the priests blew the trumpets and all Israel stood.

Solomon reigned over Israel for 40 years, and then he died.

# Elijah and the Prophets of Baal

———————— ⚭ • ⚭ ————————

After Solomon died, the nation of Israel was divided into two kingdoms, Israel and Judah. The kings of Israel were wicked, and did evil in the sight of the Lord. They made golden calves for the people to worship. Finally a king named Ahab took the throne. Ahab married Jezebel, a pagan princess. She introduced the worship of the false god Baal into Israel. Then she killed as many of the prophets of the one true God of Israel as she could find.

God sent Elijah the prophet to Ahab. Elijah had Ahab assemble all the people of Israel to Mount Carmel, along with all the prophets of Baal. Elijah had the prophets of Baal set up an altar of sacrifice. However, he directed that no fire be set to the sacrifice. He then told the false prophets to call out to their god Baal to light the fire. They called out for hours, and even cut themselves, but no one was listening. Then Elijah set up an altar to the God of Israel, poured water over his sacrifice, and called upon the Lord. The Lord sent fire from heaven which consumed the sacrifice and lapped up the water. Then the people worshipped the Lord, and Elijah put the false prophets to death.

# Elijah and the Fiery Chariot

The Lord directed Elijah to anoint Elisha as the prophet who would follow him. When the Lord was ready to take Elijah up to heaven, he and Elisha were walking together. Elijah asked Elisha to stay behind while he went on to the Jordan. "As the Lord lives, and as you yourself live," Elisha replied, "I will not leave you."

At the River Jordan, Elijah took his cloak, rolled it up and struck the water, which divided, and both crossed over on dry ground. Elijah said to Elisha, "Ask for whatever I may do for you, before I am taken from you." Elisha asked for a double portion of Elijah's spirit. Elijah replied. "If you see me taken up from you, your wish will be granted; otherwise not." Suddenly a flaming chariot and flaming horses came between them, and Elijah went up to heaven in a whirlwind. When Elisha saw this, he cried out, "My father! My father! Israel's chariots and drivers!"

Then Elisha picked up Elijah's mantle which had fallen from him, and went back and stood at the bank of the Jordan. Waving the mantle which had fallen from Elijah, he struck the water and said, "Where is the Lord, the God of Elijah?" When Elisha struck the water it divided, and he crossed over.

# The Call of Isaiah

Some years after the death of Elisha, God called a man
named Isaiah to be His prophet. Isaiah was very strong and
bold in speaking out for the Lord. He had a great reverence
for God, the "Holy One of Israel."

The kings and people of Judah had made alliances with
foreign kings. Many wars broke out as foreign kings sought
to invade their land. Finally, King Hezekiah asked Isaiah to
pray for him and help him. Thus it came to pass that the
angel of the Lord went forth and struck down the enemies
of Judah, and there was peace in the land.

Isaiah prophesied about the Messiah, the anointed one of
the Lord, who would come and deliver God's people from
all their enemies. He foretold that a virgin would be with
child, and bear a son, and she would name him Immanuel,
which means 'God with us.' He said, "For a child is born to
us, a son is given us; upon his shoulder dominion rests.
They name him Wonder-Counselor, God-Hero, Father-
Forever, and the Prince of Peace." Although he did not
realize it at the time, Isaiah was prophesying about the birth
of Jesus, our true Messiah, the Son of God, who would be
born of the Virgin Mary.

# Jonah and the Whale

⸺ ❦ ⸺

Jonah was a prophet who lived around the time of Isaiah.
One day God told Jonah, "Go to the great city of Nineveh
and preach to it, for it is very wicked." But Jonah did not
want the people of Nineveh to repent, since they were
enemies of Israel. He wanted God to punish them. So he
sailed far from there on a ship going to the city of Tarshish.

The Lord sent a great storm upon the sea. The wind was
blowing so hard that the ship was beginning to break up.
Jonah knew that it was because he was running away from
the Lord that God had sent the storm. Jonah told the
captain to have his sailors throw him overboard to bring the
storm to an end. The sailors did not know what else to do, so
they threw Jonah into the water, and the storm stopped. Then
God sent a great whale which swallowed Jonah. Jonah
begged God to free him, and after three days and nights, the
whale spit Jonah out onto dry land.

Jonah then obeyed God and preached to the people of
Nineveh. When the king and his people heard Jonah, they
realized that they had offended God. They repented of their
wickedness and turned back to God. When God saw that,
He had mercy on them, and spared their land.

# Jeremiah the Prophet

About 75 years after Isaiah, God raised up the prophet Jeremiah to bring His word to His people. In those days, King Josiah ruled over Judah. He was a good king. Jeremiah helped Josiah as he tried to reform his nation. King Josiah was killed in a war, and later a new king, Jehoiakim, came to power. He did evil in the sight of the Lord. Jeremiah prophesied against him but he would not listen. The king even burned the scroll containing the word of the Lord to Jeremiah. Thus it came to pass that Nebuchadnezzar, the king of Babylon, attacked Jerusalem and overthrew it. He then took many of the people captive into Babylon.

Jeremiah continued to speak the word of the Lord to the rest of the inhabitants of Judah, warning them that if they did not repent and return to the Lord, they would experience greater defeats. The princes of Judah did not want to hear Jeremiah, so they put him into a cistern filled with mud. He was in danger of starving to death in the cistern. However, a servant of the king rescued Jeremiah, and pulled him out of the cistern. Even though Jerusalem was destroyed, God spoke of a new beginning He would send to His people. He promised to give them a new heart.

# Daniel and the Vegetables

King Nebuchadnezzar had taken many of the Israelites captive into Babylon. He had some of the young men brought to his palace, so they could be trained to enter his service. Among these young men of Judah were Daniel and three of his friends. The king gave them food from his table, but Daniel did not want to defile himself with the food and wine, for it was unclean in the sight of the Lord. Therefore he asked to be excused from eating the king's food.

The king's steward told Daniel that the king would be angry if he saw that Daniel and his friends looked miserable compared to the other young men their age. Daniel replied, "Please give us vegetables to eat and water to drink for ten days. Then see how we look compared to the other young men who eat from the royal table." The steward agreed. After ten days Daniel and his friends looked healthier and better fed than any of the young men who ate from the royal table! The steward continued to take away the food and wine they were to receive, and gave them vegetables.

God gave knowledge and skill in all literature and science to these four young men. In addition, God gave to Daniel the understanding of all visions and dreams.

# Daniel and the Lions' Den

One night, King Nebuchadnezzar of Babylon had a very disturbing dream. Daniel was the only person who could help him understand it. The king then placed Daniel and his companions in charge of all the chief cities of Babylon.

After the death of Nebuchadnezzar, King Belshazzar gave a great banquet for a thousand of his lords. They drank out of the sacred goblets which had been taken from the Temple in Jerusalem. A hand appeared, which wrote words on the wall. The king called Daniel, who told him his kingdom would be taken from him since he had not glorified the Lord.

Later, a new king named Darius chose Daniel and two other men to help govern his kingdom. The two men were jealous of Daniel, so they convinced Darius to make a law that no one could worship any god but himself.

Daniel prayed to God and worshipped Him, as he had always done. The two men accused Daniel, and because of his law, the king threw Daniel into a den of hungry lions. However, God sent an angel to shut the mouths of the lions, and delivered His servant Daniel from the lions' den. All the people greatly honored Daniel, the servant of God.

# Esther and the King

Some time after the death of Daniel, a new king named Ahasuerus came to power in Persia. Among the Jews living there in exile was a beautiful young woman named Esther. Her cousin Mordecai served the king. The king's wife greatly displeased the king, so he divorced her and ordered his servants to find young women for his harem. He would then choose one of them to be his wife. The servants of the king chose Esther to be one of the women in the king's harem. Esther did not reveal to anyone that she was a Jew. The king loved Esther more than all the other women. He placed the royal crown on her head and made her his queen.

The king had a prime minister named Haman. Haman hated the Hebrew people, and by lying he had gained the authority to kill all the Jews in Persia. When Mordecai heard this, he told Esther that she must help her people. However, she was forbidden, under pain of death, to visit the king unless he summoned her. Esther prayed for help, and then went to see the king without being summoned. At first he was angry, but God changed his heart, and he listened to Esther. He spared the Jewish people, and punished Haman with death.

# Rebuilding the Temple

────── ❧ • ❧ ──────

The Lord inspired Cyrus, the king of Persia, to free the Jews, so they could return to Judea and rebuild the Temple in Jerusalem. Thus the first group of Jews prepared to go up to build the Temple of the Lord in Jerusalem. This group included the leaders of Judah and Benjamin as well as many priests and Levites. King Cyrus also returned the sacred vessels which had been taken from the Temple by King Nebuchadnezzar when he had defeated Jerusalem.

Joshua the high priest and Zerubbabel set about first rebuilding the altar, so they could once again offer sacrifices to the Lord. They also laid the foundations of the Temple. Then the inhabitants of the land rose up against the Jews, and hindered them in their work. Eventually, the Jews did complete the Temple and they dedicated it to the Lord.

Some time later, another king sent Ezra to lead a second group of Jews back to Judea. After him, the prophet Nehemiah brought the final group of exiles home, and they set to work rebuilding the walls around Jerusalem. Their enemies oppressed them, so they stationed guards around the city to guard it while their fellow Jews rebuilt the walls.

# Ezra and Nehemiah

When the Temple and the city of Jerusalem had been
rebuilt, all the men, women, and those children old enough
to understand gathered in a large open space in the city.
Ezra brought forth the book of the Law of Moses, which the
Lord had commanded for Israel. Ezra blessed the Lord, and
then read out of the book from dawn until noon. All the
people listened attentively to him. They began to weep when
they heard the word of the Lord, for they had forgotten it
during their exile. Then Nehemiah and Ezra said, "Today is
holy to the Lord your God. Do not be sad and do not weep.
Go, eat rich foods and drink sweet drinks, and give some to
those who have nothing; for today is holy to our Lord. The
joy of the Lord must be your strength!"

Ezra read the book of the Law for seven days. He praised
God for all that God had done for Israel. He asked God to
forgive the people for the many times they had rebelled
against Him and had disobeyed Him. The people then took
an oath to follow the Law of God. They promised to bring
offerings to Him in His holy temple. They promised to love
the Lord with all their hearts. Then they said, "Amen!"

# THE NEW TESTAMENT
## The Annunciation
— CB • BD —

Centuries passed after the Jews had returned to the land of Israel. Many of the people wondered when God would fulfill His promise to give them a Messiah. One very special day, God sent the angel Gabriel to the town of Nazareth, to a virgin named Mary, who was bethrothed to a man named Joseph. Gabriel said to Mary, "Hail, full of grace! The Lord is with you!" Mary was troubled. She did not know what sort of greeting this was.

The angel said, "Do not be afraid, Mary. You have found favor with God. Behold, you will conceive in your womb and bear a son, and you shall name him Jesus. He will be great, and will be called the Son of the Most High God. He will rule over the house of Jacob forever." Mary said, "How can this be? I am a virgin!" Gabriel replied, "The Holy Spirit will come upon you in power. Your child will be holy. And behold, Elizabeth, your cousin, has also conceived a son in her old age, for nothing will be impossible for God."

Mary said, "I am the handmaid of the Lord. Let it be done unto me according to your word." With that the angel left her.

# The Visitation

Mary set out and traveled to the hill country in haste to visit her cousin Elizabeth. When Elizabeth heard Mary's greeting, she felt the infant inside her leap in her womb. Filled with the Holy Spirit, Elizabeth cried out in a loud voice, "Most blessed are you among women, and blessed is the fruit of your womb! And how does this happen to me, that the mother of my Lord should come to me? For at the moment the sound of your greeting reached my ears, the infant in my womb leaped for joy. Blessed are you who believed that what was spoken to you by the Lord would be fulfilled."

Mary said, "My soul proclaims the greatness of the Lord. My spirit rejoices in God my savior. For He has looked upon me in my lowliness. From now on, people through all ages will call me blessed. The Mighty One has done great things for me, and holy is His name."

Mary ended by saying, "The Lord has helped Israel His servant, remembering His mercy, according to His promise to our fathers, to Abraham and to his descendants forever." Mary stayed with Elizabeth for about three months, and then returned to her home.

# The Journey to Bethlehem

Some months later, the Roman ruler, Caesar Augustus, ordered that a census be taken to find out how many people lived in the world. Everyone had to be enrolled in the town of their ancestors.

Thus, Joseph and Mary left Nazareth and journeyed to the city of David, called Bethlehem, because Joseph was of the house and family of David. It was difficult to travel because Mary was very close to her time of delivery.

Joseph and Mary arrived in Bethlehem late one night. Every inn and house of that little town was full, and they found no place to stay. Mary was very tired. Joseph and Mary trusted God, even though it was difficult. Would anyone help them?

Finally, Joseph found a stable with a manger in it. The stable was a place where the animals were kept and fed. Joseph did his best to make the stable comfortable for Mary. She laid down to rest, as the sky grew darker and the stars began to appear in all their brilliance.

# The Birth of Jesus

On that starry night, in that little stable, Mary gave birth to her son, Jesus. Mary wrapped her baby in warm clothing and laid Him in the manger.

In the fields nearby, shepherds were watching their flocks. Suddenly the angel of the Lord appeared to them and the bright glory of the Lord shone around them. The angel said to the shepherds, "Do not be afraid! Behold, I bring you good news of great joy for all people. Today in the city of David a savior has been born for you. He is Messiah and Lord. This will be a sign for you: you will find a baby wrapped in swaddling clothes and lying in a manger."

Suddenly a great number of angels appeared with the first angel. They were praising God and singing, "Glory to God in the highest, and on earth peace to men of good will." When the angels returned to heaven, the shepherds went in haste to Bethlehem. There they found Mary and Joseph, and the infant lying in the manger. When they saw this, they made known the amazing message that had been told them about the child. Then they returned home, praising God.

# The Presentation of Jesus in the Temple

 date of publication

Forty days after Jesus was born, Joseph and Mary took Him to the temple in Jerusalem to present Him to the Lord. In Jerusalem there lived an old man named Simeon, who was very good and who loved God very much. The Holy Spirit had told Simeon that he would not die until he had seen the Messiah of the Lord, the promised Redeemer.

On this day, then, the Spirit prompted Simeon to come into the Temple, where he saw Joseph, Mary, and Jesus. Simeon took the child into his arms, and he said, "Now, Master, You may let Your servant go in peace, according to Your word, for my eyes have seen Your salvation, which You prepared in sight of all the peoples, a light for revelation to the Gentiles, and glory for Your people Israel."

Simeon blessed Mary and Joseph. Then he turned to Mary and said, "This child is destined for the fall and rise of many in Israel. He shall be a sign that will be contradicted. A sword shall also pierce your own soul, so that the thoughts of many hearts may be revealed."

# The Gift of the Magi

At this time Wise Men, called Magi, traveled from afar to Jerusalem. They asked King Herod, "Where is he who is born King of the Jews? We have seen his star in the sky, and have come to worship him."

King Herod was greatly troubled when he heard this, for he was a jealous king. He did not want anyone to rule the Jews but himself. Herod asked his priests and learned men, "Where is the Messiah to be born?" They answered, "In Bethlehem, as it is written: 'You, Bethlehem, are not the least among the clans of Judah; since from you shall come a ruler who is to shepherd my people Israel.'"

Then Herod called the travelers secretly, and asked them what time they had seen the star in the sky. He sent them to Bethlehem, and told them to search for the child.

The Magi set out, following the star until it stopped over the place where Jesus was. They found Jesus with Mary His mother. They worshiped Him, and gave Him gifts of gold, frankincense, and myrrh. The Magi did not return to Herod, but left for home by another way.

# The Flight Into Egypt

When the Magi departed, the angel of the Lord appeared to Joseph in a dream. "Get up Joseph!" the angel said. "Take the child and His mother and flee to Egypt, because King Herod is searching for the child to kill Him!" Joseph took Mary and Jesus that very night into Egypt.

They remained in Egypt until the death of Herod. Meanwhile, Herod had ordered his soldiers to kill all the boys in Bethlehem who were two years old and younger. There was a loud weeping in Bethlehem, as mothers and fathers mourned their children who were taken from them.

After a time, Herod died, and the angel appeared in a dream again to Joseph. "Rise," the angel said. "Take the child and His mother and return to Israel, for those who sought the child's life are dead."

Joseph rose, and took his little family back to Nazareth. And thus it was that what the prophets had spoken of the Messiah came to be fulfilled: "He shall be called a Nazorean."

# Jesus Grows Up

— ☙ • ❧ —

The town of Nazareth was hilly, and one hill was quite high. Jesus might have climbed that very hill as a boy. On a clear day, He could see Mount Carmel, where Elijah the prophet had called down fire from heaven. From the hilltop, Jesus could also glimpse the Sea of Galilee, with its shimmering blue water reflecting sparkles from the sun.

Joseph worked hard building and repairing homes, and making plows, tables, and other items. Mary prepared meals, cleaned, sewed clothes, tended the garden, and took good care of her husband and son.

Jesus learned to read, write, and to work a trade with his father Joseph. Every Saturday, the family celebrated the Sabbath, a day set aside for the worship of the God of Israel and for a rest. Mary gathered the family around her and lit the Sabbath candles. Joseph intoned the Sabbath prayers.

In Nazareth, Jesus came to know rich people and poor people, good people and bad people. As He grew, Jesus also learned to hear the voice of His heavenly Father. The time for His mission was drawing near.

# The Finding of Jesus in the Temple

Every year Joseph and Mary took Jesus with them to Jerusalem for the feast of Passover, as God had commanded the Jews when He delivered them from Egypt. When Jesus was twelve years old, He went up to Jerusalem with His parents as usual. Afterwards, they returned home, but Jesus remained behind without their knowing it.

When Joseph and Mary realized that Jesus was missing, they returned to Jerusalem to look for Him. After three days they finally found Jesus in the temple, sitting with the teachers and priests, listening to them and asking them questions. Everyone who heard Jesus was amazed at His understanding.

Mary said, "Son, why have You done this to us? Your father and I have looked for You with sorrow!" Jesus answered, "Did you not know I must be in my Father's house?" Mary and Joseph did not understand His answer. Then Jesus returned to Nazareth with His parents, and He obeyed them in all things. Mary kept all these words in her heart. Meanwhile, Jesus grew in wisdom, age, and favor before God and all the people.

# The Baptism of Jesus

When Jesus was 30 years old, He left His home in Nazareth. He came to the Jordan River to be baptized by His cousin John. John the Baptist lived in the desert, where he spent much time in prayer. John wore a garment of camel's skin, and ate only grasshoppers and wild honey. John was baptizing the people in the river Jordan for the forgiveness of sins. When he saw Jesus, John was unwilling to baptize Him, for he knew He was holy. But Jesus told John to do so, because that was what God wanted.

After Jesus was baptized, suddenly the sky opened up, and John saw the Holy Spirit in the shape of a dove come down from heaven and rest upon Jesus. The people around heard a voice from heaven, which said, "This is my Beloved Son, in whom I am well pleased."

John the Baptist said, "Behold the Lamb of God, who takes away the sin of the world. The One who sent me to baptize told me, 'When you see the Holy Spirit descend like a dove on someone, it is he who will baptize with the Holy Spirit.' Now I have seen and testify that Jesus is the Son of God."

# The Temptation in the Desert

The Holy Spirit led Jesus into the desert, where the devil tempted Him. Jesus fasted from food for forty days and forty nights. The devil said, "If you are the Son of God, command that these stones become loaves of bread." Jesus replied, "It is written: 'Man does not live by bread alone, but by every word that comes forth from the mouth of God.'"

The devil then took Jesus to the roof of the Temple. "If you are the Son of God, throw yourself down," he said. "It is written, 'God will command his angels concerning you' and 'they will support you with their hands, lest you dash your foot against a stone.'" Jesus replied, "It is also written, 'You shall not put the Lord, your God, to the test.'"

Then the devil took Jesus up to a very high mountain, and showed Him all the kingdoms of the world. He offered to give them to Jesus if Jesus would worship him. Jesus said, "Begone, Satan! It is written: 'You shall worship the Lord your God, and him alone shall you serve.'" Then the devil left Jesus and angels came and served Him.

# Jesus Calls His Apostles

Jesus returned from the desert filled with the Holy Spirit and power. John the Baptist saw Him and said, "Behold the Lamb of God!" Two of John's disciples, Andrew and John, followed after Jesus. He turned and said, "What are you looking for?" They asked Him, "Teacher, where are you staying?" Jesus replied, "Come and see."

Andrew told his brother Peter about Jesus, and John told his brother James as well. Later, Jesus found these men by the Sea of Galilee, for they were fishermen. He said to them, "Come follow me, and I will make you fishers of men." At once they left their nets and followed Jesus. Jesus called other men to follow Him as well, and soon He had twelve apostles.

The names of the twelve apostles are: Peter and Andrew; James and John; Philip and Bartholomew; Thomas and Matthew, James, Simon and Jude, and Judas Iscariot, who betrayed the Lord.

# The Wedding at Cana

There was a wedding in the town of Cana in Galilee, and Mary, the mother of Jesus was there. Jesus and His disciples had also been invited to the wedding. When Mary saw that the hosts were running out of wine, she said to Jesus, "They have no more wine." Jesus replied, "Woman, what is that to me and to you? My hour has not yet come." Still, Mary believed that Jesus would act to help the hosts, so she told the servers, "Do whatever he tells you."

In the banquet room there were six large stone jars, and Jesus told the servants, "Fill the jars with water." Then Jesus said, "Draw some out and take it to the headwaiter." The headwaiter tasted the water, which had become wine. He told the groom, "Usually people serve the good wine first, and then, when people have drunk a lot, they serve the lesser wine. But you have kept the good wine until now."

Jesus worked this miracle as the first of His signs. In this manner He revealed His glory, and His disciples began to believe in Him. After this, Jesus and His mother, His brethren, and His disciples went down to Capernaum, near the Sea of Galilee. They stayed there a few days, and then it was time to move on.

# Jesus Cleanses the Temple

Since the Passover celebration of the Jews was near, Jesus went up to the temple in Jerusalem. He found in the temple area those who sold oxen, sheep, and doves, as well as the money-changers. Jesus made a whip and drove them all out of the temple, with their sheep and oxen. He turned over the tables of the money-changers and spilled their coins. He said to those selling doves, "Take these out of here, and stop making my Father's house a marketplace!"

When the disciples of Jesus saw this, they remembered the words of scripture, "Zeal for your house will consume me." Meanwhile, the Jews were angry at Jesus. They said to Him, "What sign can you show us for doing this?"

Jesus answered, "Destroy this temple and in three days I will raise it up." The Jews said, "It took forty-six years to build this temple. How are you going to raise it up in three days?" They did not understand that Jesus was speaking about the temple of His body. Therefore, when Jesus was raised from the dead, His disciples remembered that He had said this, and they came to believe the scripture and the word which Jesus had spoken.

# Nicodemus Comes to Jesus

In Israel there was a ruler of the Jews named Nicodemus. He came to Jesus one night, when no one was watching. He said, "Rabbi, we know that you are a teacher who has come from God. No one can do these signs that you are doing unless God is with him."

Jesus said, "Truly, no one can see the kingdom of God unless he is born from above."

Nicodemus asked Jesus, "How can a person who has grown old be born again?"

Jesus responded, "Truly I say to you, no one can enter the kingdom of God without being born of water and Spirit. You must be born from above."

Nicodemus wondered how this could happen. Jesus answered, "You are the teacher of Israel and you do not understand this? Amen, amen, I say to you, no one has gone up to heaven except the one who has come down from heaven, the Son of Man. For God so loved the world that he gave his only Son, so that everyone who believes in him might not perish but might have eternal life."

# The Woman at the Well

One day Jesus traveled with His disciples through Samaria to a place called Jacob's well. Jews and Samaritans did not share anything in common. A Samaritan woman came to the well to fill up her water pitcher. Jesus asked for a drink. She replied, "How can you, a Jew, ask me for a drink?"

Jesus replied, "If you knew who I was, you would ask me for living water."

"Sir," the woman responded, "you don't even have a bucket. Where will you get this living water?"

Jesus answered, "Everyone who drinks this water will be thirsty again; but whoever drinks the water I shall give will never thirst. The water I shall give will become in him a spring of water welling up to eternal life."

When the woman asked for the living water, Jesus told her to call her husband first. She answered that she had none. Jesus answered her, "You are right. You have had five husbands, and the one you have now is not your husband." The woman realized that Jesus knew all about her. She came to believe in Him, and because of her, many Samaritans also began to believe that Jesus was the Messiah.

# Jesus Heals Peter's Mother-in-Law

Jesus and His disciples came to Capernaum, a town on the edge of the Sea of Galilee. He stayed at the home of Simon Peter, who lived there.

The Jewish people worked six days a week, but rested on the Sabbath. They worshipped God on the Sabbath, in their synagogues. A synagogue was a house of prayer where the Jews would gather to worship God and to hear the Law of Moses and the Scriptures.

On the Sabbath Jesus entered the synagogue at Capernaum and taught. The people were astonished at His teaching, for He taught them with authority and confidence. They felt good about this teacher. They listened to His words and wanted to hear more.

When Jesus left the synagogue He went back to the home of Simon Peter. Simon's mother-in-law lay sick in bed with a fever. They immediately told Him about her. Jesus walked over to the sick woman. He grasped her hand and helped her up. Then the fever left her and she waited on them.

# Jesus Heals After Sunset

When it was evening, after sunset on the Sabbath, the people of Capernaum were free to leave their homes and move around again, because the Sabbath was over. When they heard that Jesus had healed Peter's mother-in-law, everyone was excited. They asked each other, "Will Jesus be able to heal our sick friends too?"

So they began to gather outside the door of Peter's home. There were mothers who brought their babies to be healed. Other people brought their friends who were blind. Some people were lame or could not walk very well. Other people had different types of diseases. Some people were troubled by demons and dark spirits. Some of the sick had not been outside of their homes for a long time!

The whole town gathered at the door. Jesus cured many who were sick with various diseases, and He drove out many demons. He did not permit the demons to speak, because they knew that He was the Messiah.

Jesus went into the synagogues throughout Capernaum and all of Galilee. He preached to the people, drove out demons, and healed the sick. Truly, God was visiting His people!

# Jesus Cures a Leper

As Jesus walked along, a leper approached and knelt down before Him. Leprosy was a serious illness that caused the skin of a person to become white and fall off. Lepers had to stay away from everyone, and call out, "Unclean! Unclean!"

"Please, Lord," the leper said, "if you wish, you can make me clean." Jesus felt pity for the man. He stretched out His hand and touched him, and said, "I will do it. Be made clean." The leprosy left the man immediately. He was healed!

Jesus then told the man sternly, "Tell no one, but go, show yourself to the priest, and offer for your cleansing the gift that Moses prescribed. That will be proof for them."

The Law of Moses required the priests to inspect lepers. Once a leper was declared clean, the person could offer sacrifices to God and could live close to other people again.

The man left and told everyone how Jesus had healed him. So many people heard about the cure that Jesus was unable to enter a town openly. He remained outside in deserted places, and people came to Him from everywhere.

# Jesus Heals a Paralytic

One day Jesus was preaching in a home in Capernaum. So many people crowded the home that no one else could enter. Some men arrived, carrying a man who was so badly paralyzed that he lay on a mat. Since they were not able to get inside the house, they decided to go up on the roof! They took off some of the roof tiles, made a hole in the ceiling, and let down the man right in front of Jesus.

Jesus was so pleased at their faith that He said to the sick man, "Son, your sins are forgiven." Some of the religious leaders thought to themselves, "Who but God alone can forgive sins?" Jesus said, "Which is easier to say, 'Your sins are forgiven,' or 'Arise, take up your bed, and walk?'" To show that He had authority to forgive sins on earth, Jesus said to the paralytic, "Rise, pick up your mat, and go home." The people waited to see what would happen. The man stood up, picked up his bed, and walked away in the sight of everyone, thanking Jesus, and praising God. The people were totally amazed, and they gave glory to God, saying, "We have never seen anything like this!"

# Jesus Calls Matthew

As Jesus passed on from there, he saw a man named Matthew. Matthew worked for the pagan Romans. He sat at a table, collecting taxes from the people. The people did not like tax collectors. They looked down on them. Jesus said to Matthew, "Follow me." Matthew stood up right away. He left his tax table and began to follow Jesus.

Jesus then went to eat at Matthew's home. While He was sitting at table in Matthew's house, many other tax collectors and sinners came and sat with Jesus and His disciples. The Pharisees saw this. The Pharisees were religious leaders who separated themselves from anyone who was a sinner or who was not Jewish. They said to the disciples of Jesus, "Why does your teacher eat with tax collectors and sinners?"

Jesus heard what the Pharisees asked His disciples. He turned to them and said, "Those who are well do not need a doctor, but the sick do. Go and learn the meaning of the words, 'I desire mercy, not sacrifice.' I did not come to call people who think they are good. I came to call sinners."

# The Pool of Bethesda

Jesus and His disciples went up to Jerusalem. In Jerusalem there was a pool of water called the Pool of Bethesda. At times, the water would bubble up. The people believed that the first person into the pool when it bubbled would be cured. Many sick, lame, and blind people used to wait near the pool, hoping to be cured.

One poor man had been at the pool for 38 years. He was paralyzed, and needed help moving over to the pool. It took him so long to move that whenever the water was stirred up, someone else would get into the pool before him. When Jesus heard about this man, He asked him, "Do you want to be well?" The sick man answered, "Sir, I have no one to help me get in the water after it is stirred up. While I am on my way, someone goes down there before me."

Jesus said to the man, "Arise, take up your mat, and walk." Immediately the man became well, and he took up his mat and walked! Later, Jesus found the man in the temple area. He told him, "Do not sin anymore, so that nothing worse may happen to you."

# The Sermon on the Mount

One day Jesus went up a mountain to teach His disciples and the people about God. He said to them, "Blessed are those who are poor, who trust in God, for theirs is the kingdom of heaven. Blessed are those who mourn and are sad, for God will comfort them. Blessed are the meek, those who are humble, for the earth will be given to them. Blessed are those who hunger to be good and to know the goodness of God, for they shall be satisfied. Blessed are those who help others with mercy, for mercy shall be theirs. Blessed are the pure of heart, for they will see God. Blessed are those who make peace, for they shall be called the children of God. Blessed are those who suffer for doing what is right, for the kingdom of heaven belongs to them."

Jesus also said, "You are the salt of the earth. God wants to do good work through you. You are the light of the world. God wants your light to shine so that people may see the good you do and give glory to your heavenly Father. Seek first the kingdom of God, and everything else will be given to you." The people listened eagerly to Jesus, who told them the truth. When He came down the mountain, great crowds followed Him, for He taught with authority.

# Jesus Heals the Centurion's Servant
— ⚜ • ⚜ —

When Jesus came down from the mountain, He entered
Capernaum. A Roman officer, who was called a centurion,
had a slave who was very sick. The centurion went up to Jesus
and asked Him to help. "Lord," he said, "my servant is lying
at home. He cannot move, and he is suffering terribly." Jesus
said, "I will come and cure him."

The centurion replied, "Lord, I am not worthy to have you
enter under my roof. Only say the word and my servant will be
healed." He looked at Jesus with expectant faith.

When Jesus heard this, He was amazed. He said to those
following Him, "Truly I tell you, I have not found such faith in
any one in Israel. Many will come from the east and the west,
and will sit with Abraham, Isaac, and Jacob at the banquet in
the kingdom of heaven. However, the children of the kingdom
will be driven out into the outer darkness."

Jesus to the centurion, "You may go. Let it be done for you as
you have believed." At that very hour the centurion's servant
was healed.

# Jesus Calms the Storm

One day, Jesus taught by the Sea of Galilee. He spoke for a long time. He healed many people. At the end of the day, as the evening drew near, Jesus said, "Let us cross to the other side." His disciples took Him and began to cross the sea. Jesus was very tired, so He curled up in the boat and fell fast asleep.

Suddenly a violent storm came up on the sea. The waves grew higher and higher. They began to wash over the boat and to fill it with water. The disciples did their best to stay afloat, but when they realized the boat was sinking, they felt terrified. They went to Jesus and woke Him up. "Lord," they cried, "save us! We are perishing!"

Jesus said to them, "Why are you afraid? Do you not yet have faith? Then He stood up and rebuked the wind. He said to the sea, "Quiet! Be still!"

Suddenly the rains stopped falling, the winds stopped blowing, and the sea grew calm. The disciples looked at each other in amazement. "What sort of man is this?" they asked. "Even the winds and the sea obey Him!"

# Jesus Heals a Little Girl

When the boat came to shore, people gathered around Jesus and He taught them. Suddenly a man named Jairus rushed up. He was a ruler in the synagogue. Jairus fell down on his knees before Jesus and cried, "My only little girl, who is just twelve years old, is dying. Please, Jesus, come and heal her!"

Jesus rose up and followed Jairus. As they came near to the home, some people said to Jairus, "Do not bother Jesus anymore. Your daughter is dead." Jesus turned to Jairus and said to him, "Be not afraid. Just have faith."

When they came to the house, many people were crying and wailing loudly. Jesus said, "Do not weep. The child is not dead but asleep." Some of the people made fun of Jesus because of what He said. Jesus had them put out. Then He took His closest apostles, Peter, James, and John, into the room, with Jairus and his wife. Jesus walked up to the bed and took the girl by the hand. He said, "Little girl, I say to you, arise!" Immediately the little girl got up and began to walk around. When the people saw what Jesus had done, they were completely amazed.

# The Miracle of the Loaves and Fishes

Many people came from all over Israel, sometimes traveling for days, just to listen to Jesus. They knew He was very special. One time more than 5,000 people had been with Him all day, and they were hungry. The apostles were worried because they had no food for them. They wanted to send the people home, but they knew that many of them lived far away.

The apostles told Jesus, "Send the people away that they may go to the towns and buy food." Jesus answered, "Give them food yourselves to eat." The disciples replied, "There is a boy here who has five loaves of bread and two fish, but what good are these for so many?"

Jesus said, "Have the people sit down in groups of fifty." Then He took the loaves and the fish, looked up to heaven, and blessed them. Jesus gave them to His disciples to give to the people. Everyone ate their fill of the loaves and fish. When they were done, the disciples collected twelve baskets of leftovers! Just as Jesus had promised, God always provides us what we need when we put our trust in Him.

# Jesus Walks on the Water

After Jesus had fed the people with the loaves and the fishes, He told His disciples to take the boat across the Sea of Galilee and wait for Him. Jesus sent the people back to their homes. Then He went up into the mountains by Himself to pray. Jesus loved to pray alone to His Father, especially on mountains or out in the desert. He loved to take time to be with His Father, for He loved the Father, and the Father loved Him.

As the disciples waited for Jesus out on the sea, the winds arose. The waves began to fall and rise, higher and higher. They were crashing in on the apostles. They tried their best to keep the boat afloat. Jesus saw His disciples out in the boat by themselves. He knew they were afraid.

Jesus climbed down the mountain and walked to the sea. Then He stepped out on the waves. He began to walk on the water toward the boat. When the disciples saw Jesus walking toward them on the water in the middle of the night, they cried out in fear, "It is a ghost!"

Jesus said, "It is I. Be not afraid."

# Jesus Rescues Peter

The disciples saw Jesus coming near them. They heard Him say, "It is I. Be not afraid." But they had never seen anyone walk on water before. Was it really Jesus?

Peter then called out from the boat, "Lord, if it is you, command me to come to you!" "Come," Jesus said. Peter stepped out of the boat and began to walk on the water towards Jesus. As long as he looked at Jesus, he was able to walk. However, when Peter looked at the sea, and saw how rough it was, and how hard the winds were blowing, he began to sink. Peter cried out, "Lord, save me!"

Jesus immediately stretched out His hand to catch Peter. He said to him, "O you of little faith! Why did you doubt?" After Jesus and Peter got into the boat, the winds died down and the sea grew calm. The disciples in the boat were completely amazed. They worshiped Jesus and said to Him, "Truly, You are the Son of God!"

# Jesus Names Peter as the Rock

 G3 • ह0

Jesus traveled up and down the land of Israel, preaching the Gospel to the Jewish people. He healed the people and taught them about the Kingdom of God.

One day Jesus asked His disciples, who followed Him, "Who do people say that the Son of Man is?" They replied, "Some say you are John the Baptist, or Elijah, or one of the prophets." Jesus then asked them, "But who do you say that I am?" The apostles were silent. Then Simon Peter replied, "You are the Messiah, the Son of the living God."

Jesus said, "Blessed are you, Simon son of Jonah. For flesh and blood has not revealed this to you, but my heavenly Father. And so I say to you, you are Peter, and upon this rock I will build my church, and the gates of hell shall not prevail against it. The gates of hell shall not hold out against my church. I will give you the keys to the kingdom of heaven. Whatever you bind on earth shall be bound in heaven, and whatever you loose on earth shall be loosed in heaven."

Jesus then strictly ordered His disciples to tell no one that He was the Messiah.

# The Transfiguration of the Lord

One day Jesus took Peter, James, and John with Him up on a high mountain. When they reached the top, suddenly Jesus' face began to shine like the sun! The light that was shining out of Jesus and all around Him was so bright that His robes became as white as snow. His disciples looked at Jesus in amazement. Suddenly, Moses and Elijah appeared and began talking to Jesus. As you may remember, Moses led the Israelites out of Egypt and gave them the Law. Elijah was a great prophet who had lived many years before Jesus.

Peter offered to make three tents for Jesus, Moses, and Elijah. While he was still speaking, a bright cloud appeared, casting a shadow around them, and a voice from the cloud spoke, and said, "This is my beloved Son, in whom I am well pleased. Listen to him." When the disciples heard this, they fell flat on the ground in fear. Jesus went over and touched them, saying, "Arise, be not afraid."

Peter, James, and John looked up, and they saw no one but Jesus. They walked down the mountain together, and Jesus told them to tell no one what had happened, until He had risen from the dead.

# Jesus Blesses the Children

Little children loved to be around Jesus because they knew He loved them. His warm smile and big hugs made them feel good. And Jesus loved the little children. He liked telling them stories about farmers and fishermen, shepherds and kings. He would listen to the children, and they would listen to Him.

One day some mothers and fathers brought their children to Jesus so that He might lay His hands on them and bless them. The apostles cried, "Stop! Jesus is too busy to see your children!" But Jesus said, "Let the children come to me, and do not stop them. My kingdom belongs to such as these. Unless you become like little children, you shall not enter the kingdom of heaven."

Then all the children ran up to Jesus. They laughed as He smiled at them, hugged them, and spoke with them. Jesus blessed the children and gave them back to their parents. When the children grew up, they remembered the Wonderful Storyteller who had loved them so much, and they followed Him.

# The Good Samaritan

One day, while Jesus was teaching, a student of the Law asked Him, "What must I do to receive eternal life?" Jesus replied, "You must love the Lord your God with all your heart, and love your neighbor as you love yourself."

"But who is my neighbor?" asked the lawyer. Jesus replied, "A man was going down from Jerusalem to Jericho when suddenly, robbers attacked him. They stripped and beat him and left him half-dead. A priest passed by, but when he saw him, he passed on the opposite side. Likewise a Levite came by, who also passed him by. But a Samaritan traveler was moved with compassion when he saw the wounded man. He poured oil and wine over his wounds and bandaged them. Then he lifted him up on his own donkey, took him to an inn and cared for him. He gave money to the innkeeper, and said, 'Take care of him. If you spend more, I shall repay you when I return.'"

"Who do you think was neighbor to the man?" Jesus asked. The scholar answered, "The one who treated him with mercy." Jesus said to him, "Then go and do the same."

# The Good Shepherd

Jesus said, "Once upon a time there was a shepherd who had many sheep. He knew each of them by name. Every day he took them out into the fields and meadows so they could eat good rich grass and drink cool water.

"One day, a little lamb ran away from the rest of the sheep and got lost. When the shepherd realized his lamb was missing, he left his other sheep and went to find it. He looked up in the mountains and down by the streams. Finally he found the frightened little lamb, put it on his shoulders, and brought it home. The shepherd said, 'Rejoice with me, for I have found my sheep that was lost!'"

Jesus said, "I am the Good Shepherd. I know my sheep, and they know me, and they follow me. If they get lost, I search for them and find them and bring them back home to me." Jesus wanted the people to know that each one of them belonged to Him, like a sheep belongs to a shepherd. If a person makes a bad choice and does something wrong, like the little lamb that ran away, Jesus goes to find that person, and He brings him back to Himself. Jesus laid down His life for all people on Calvary, to bring us all back to Him.

# Jesus Teaches His Disciples to Pray

Jesus loved to go away to quiet places and pray. His disciples saw how deeply He loved God His Father. They wanted to love God the same way. And so, one day, when Jesus had finished praying, one of His followers said, "Lord, teach us to pray."

Jesus answered, "When you pray, say, 'Our Father, who art in heaven, hallowed be Thy name. Thy kingdom come, Thy will be done, on earth as it is in heaven.

"Give us this day our daily bread, and forgive us our sins as we forgive those who sin against us, and do not put us to the test, but deliver us from the evil one.'"

Jesus said, "If you forgive others, your heavenly Father will forgive you. But if you do not forgive others, neither will your Father forgive you for what you do. And I tell you, ask and you will receive; seek and you will find; knock and the door will be opened to you. For everyone who asks, receives; and the one who seeks, finds; and to the one who knocks, the door will be opened."

The disciples of Jesus prayed as Jesus had taught them, and they taught His prayer to all those who would follow Him.

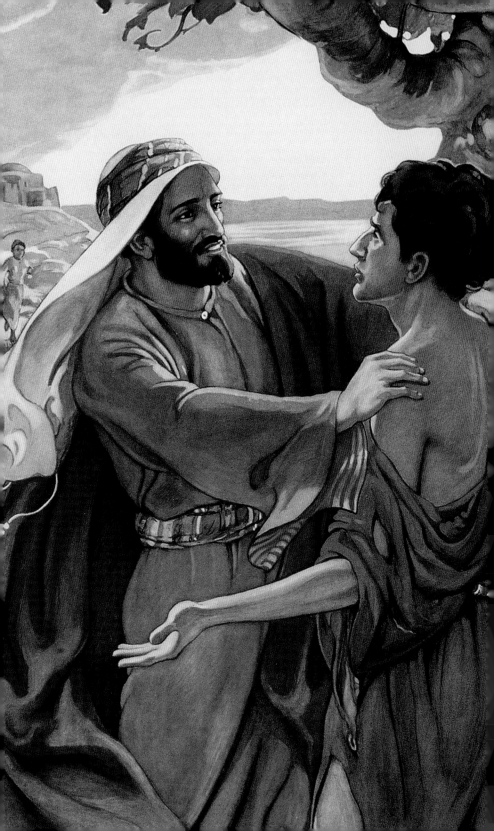

# The Forgiving Father

Jesus loved all people and reached out to them, including those who had sinned and had wandered far from God. When the religious leaders saw this, they accused Jesus of welcoming sinners and eating with them.

Jesus told them this story: "A rich man had two sons. The younger son said, 'Father, give me my share of your estate. I want to leave home.'

"The father was sad, but he gave the son his share. The younger son left and spent all his money. He finally found a job feeding pigs. He longed to eat their food, but nobody gave him anything. He thought, 'My father's servants have all they want to eat, but I am starving! I shall return to my father and say, "I have sinned and do not deserve to be called your son. Treat me as one of your servants."'

"And so the son started for home. While he was still a long way off, his father saw him. He was so happy that he ran to his son, hugged him and kissed him. He said to his servants, 'Give him the finest robe, and put a ring on his finger and sandals on his feet. Let's have a big party, because my son was dead, and has come to life. He was lost, and is found!'"

# The Rich Man and Lazarus

— Cʒ • ᴃꝺ —

Jesus told another story: "Once upon a time, there lived a very rich man. He wore nice clothes, ate delicious food, and drank fine wine every day. At his door there lay a very poor man named Lazarus. He was so sick that the dogs came and licked his sores. Lazarus was so hungry that he would gladly have eaten the scraps that fell from the rich man's table. However, the rich man did not even give him a crumb.

"Lazarus died, and the angels took him to Paradise, where he rested in Abraham's arms. Later, the rich man also died, but he went down to hell. From there, he raised his eyes and saw Abraham, with Lazarus at his side. He cried out, 'Father Abraham, have pity on me! Send Lazarus to dip the tip of his finger in water and cool my tongue, for I am suffering in these flames!'

"Abraham replied, 'My son, you received good things during your life, while Lazarus received what was bad. Now he is comforted, while you are tormented. Besides, there is a great gulf between us, to prevent anyone from crossing over.' The rich man said, 'I beg you, father, send Lazarus from the dead to warn my brothers.' But Abraham replied, 'If they will not listen to Moses and the prophets, neither will they listen even if someone should rise from the dead.'"

# Jesus Raises Lazarus From the Dead

There was a village near Jerusalem named Bethany. Jesus had some good friends who lived there, named Martha, Mary, and their brother Lazarus. One day Martha and Mary sent word to Jesus that Lazarus was very ill.

When Jesus and His disciples arrived, they found that Lazarus was already dead. He had been in the tomb for four days. Martha said to Jesus, "Lord, if you had been here, my brother would not have died. But even now, I know that whatever you ask of God, He will give you." Jesus said, "I am the resurrection and the life. Whoever believes in me, even if he dies, will live; and he who lives and believes in me will never die. Do you believe this?" "Yes, Lord," Martha said, "I have come to believe that you are the Messiah, the Son of God, the one who is to come into the world."

Jesus came to the tomb. "Take away the stone," He ordered. Jesus raised His eyes to heaven and said, "Father, I thank You for hearing me. You always hear me." Then Jesus cried out in a loud voice, "Lazarus, come forth!" Suddenly the dead man stumbled out of the tomb, wrapped in burial cloths. "Untie him," said Jesus, "and let him go."

# The Pharisee and the Publican
— ⅏ • ⅏ —

Jesus liked to tell stories, called parables, to the people. The people liked the parables, because Jesus used them to tell the truth in an unexpected way.

One day Jesus directed a parable to a group of people called the Pharisees. Many of them trusted in themselves. They believed that they were without blame. They looked down on everyone else. Jesus said, "Two men went up to the temple area to pray. One was a Pharisee and the other was a tax collector. The Pharisee stood up at the front of the temple, and spoke this prayer to himself: 'O God,' he said, 'I thank you that I am not like other men. They are greedy, dishonest, and impure. I thank you that I am not even like this tax collector. I fast twice a week, and I give you contributions from my whole income.'

"The tax collector stood far off. He did even lift his eyes to heaven, but he beat his breast and prayed, 'O God, be merciful to me a sinner.' I tell you, the tax collector went home justified, but not the Pharisee. Everyone who exalts himself will be humbled, but he who humbles himself will be exalted."

# Zacchaeus

One day Jesus came to a town called Jericho. It was near Jerusalem. He intended to pass through the town. Now there lived in Jericho a man named Zacchaeus. He was a chief tax collector and he had a lot of money. He wanted to see who Jesus was, but he could not because he was too short. So, in order to see over the crowd, Zacchaeus ran ahead and climbed a tree.

When Jesus passed by the tree, He looked up and said, "Zacchaeus, come down quickly! Today I must stay at your house." Zacchaeus could hardly believe his ears. "Jesus wants to visit me!" he thought. He climbed down the tree quickly and received Jesus with joy into his home.

Meanwhile, the people began to whisper to each other, "Jesus has gone to stay at the home of a sinner." But Zacchaeus stood there and said to the Lord, "Behold, Lord, I will give half of my money to the poor. If I have taken anything from anyone I shall repay it four times over." Jesus said to him, "Today salvation has come to this house, because this man too is a child of Abraham. For the Son of Man has come to seek and save that which was lost."

# Blind Bartimaeus

As Jesus and His disciples were leaving Jericho, a crowd of people followed Him. By the roadside there sat a blind man named Bartimaeus, the son of Timaeus. He used to beg for money from those who passed by. Bartimaeus heard the sound of the voices in the crowd. He asked someone what was happening. "Jesus is passing by," they told him.

Bartimaeus cried out, "Jesus, Son of David, have pity on me!" "Be quiet!" the people told him. "You are making too much noise." But Bartimaeus cried out even louder, "Jesus, Son of David, have pity on me! Please help me!"

Jesus stopped. "Call the man," He said. The people went over and called Bartimaeus, saying, "Take courage; get up. Jesus wants to see you." Bartimaeus threw aside his cloak, stood up, and had his friends take him over to Jesus.

Jesus looked at Bartimaeus, and asked, "What do you want me to do for you?" Bartimaeus lifted his head, and said, "Master, I want to see." Jesus smiled at Bartimaeus, and said, "Go your way, my friend. Your faith has saved you." Immediately Bartimaeus' eyes opened, and he was able to see. He rejoiced and shouted, "I can see! I can see!" Then he followed Jesus on the way.

# The Parable of the Ten Virgins

————— ○ ● ○ —————

In the time of Jesus, weddings were held at the home of the bride. Afterwards, the bridegroom would lead a procession to his home, where there would be a great feast. The bridesmaids would wait outside the home of the bridegroom until he arrived, and then would go in with him to the feast.

"The kingdom of heaven," Jesus said, "will be like ten virgins who were bridesmaids. Each of them took lamps and went out to wait for the groom. Five of them were foolish and five of them were wise. The foolish ones did not bring any extra oil with them. The wise maids brought flasks of oil with their lamps. Since the bridegroom took a long time in arriving, they all fell asleep. At midnight someone cried, 'The bridegroom is here! Come out to meet him!'

"The wise virgins put oil in their lamps, but the foolish said, 'Give us some of your oil, for our lamps are going out.' The wise ones replied, 'There may not be enough for us and you. Go and buy some for yourselves.' While they were gone, the bridegroom came and the wise maidens went in to the wedding feast with him. Then the door was locked. When the other maidens returned they cried, 'Lord, Lord, open the door!' But he replied, 'I do not know you.' Therefore, stay awake, for you do not know when I will come for you."

# Jesus Enters Jerusalem

Jesus said to His apostles, "It is time for us to go to Jerusalem. The feast of the Passover is near." Jesus sent two disciples, saying to them, "Go into the nearby village, where you will find a donkey tied up, that no one has ever ridden. Untie it and bring it here to me. If anyone should say anything to you, tell them, 'The Master needs it.'"

The two disciples found the donkey and brought it to Jesus. They covered it with their cloaks, and helped Him to mount. As they headed into Jerusalem, a great crowd that had come to the feast heard that Jesus was coming. They were very excited and went out to meet Him.

Some of the people laid their cloaks and clothes on the ground where Jesus was passing. Others cut down palm branches to lay before Him. As Jesus drew near Jerusalem, riding the donkey, His disciples and the crowd began to praise God joyfully for all the great and wonderful deeds they had seen Jesus do. Many men, women, and children waved palm and olive branches as Jesus passed by, crying out, "Hosanna! Blessed is He who comes in the name of the Lord! Hosanna!" They all entered Jerusalem with great joy.

# Jesus Washes the Feet of His Apostles

On the night of the Passover, Jesus sat down with His apostles for the Passover meal. The devil had already put it into the heart of Judas Iscariot to betray Jesus. Jesus got up from the supper, took a towel and wrapped it around His waist. He then poured water into a basin and began to wash the apostles' feet and dry them with the towel.

Jesus came to Simon Peter, who said, "Master, are you going to wash my feet?" Jesus answered that someday Peter would understand what He was doing. Jesus said, "You call me teacher, which is right, for so I am. If I, the master and teacher, wash your feet, you also ought to wash one another's feet. As I have done for you, you should also do."

After Jesus had washed His apostles' feet, He returned to the table. Then He said, "Truly I tell you, one of you is about to betray me." The disciples were hurt to hear this. Each of them asked sorrowfully, "Is it I, Lord?" Finally Judas Iscariot said, "Surely it is not I, Teacher?"

Jesus looked at him and said, "You have said so." Then Judas left. And it was night.

# The Last Supper

―――――― ☙ • ❧ ――――――

While they were eating the Passover meal, Jesus took the bread, blessed it, broke it, and gave it to His disciples saying, "Take and eat; this is my body."

Then He took a cup that was filled with wine, gave thanks, and passed it around, saying, "Drink this, all of you, for this is my blood, to be poured out for the forgiveness of sins. Do this in memory of me."

Jesus said to His disciples, "Tonight all of you will have your faith in me put to the test, and you will all be scattered. But after I have been raised up, I will go before you into Galilee."

Peter went up to Jesus and said, "Even if everyone else has their faith in you shaken, my faith will never be shaken." Jesus said to him, "Peter, truly I tell you, this very night, before the rooster crows, you will deny me three times." But Peter refused to believe Jesus, and he said again that he would never deny Him. The other apostles said the same thing.

Jesus and His apostles then sang a hymn of praise to God, and went out to the Mount of Olives.

# The Agony in the Garden

Jesus went out with His disciples to the Garden of Gethsemane. He took Peter, James, and John, with Him further, and He became very sad and troubled. Jesus asked them to stay awake and pray. Then He moved away a little bit and knelt down, praying, "Father, if You are willing, You can take this suffering away from me. Yet let it not be what I will, but what You will."

Jesus prayed very hard for the strength to do what His Father wanted Him to do. Then He went back to His disciples, but they had all fallen asleep. Jesus said to Peter, "Could you not watch one hour with me? Watch and pray, that you may not undergo the test. The spirit is willing, but the flesh is weak!"

Judas Iscariot, the apostle who had left the Last Supper, came into the garden with a crowd of soldiers. He kissed Jesus. Jesus said, "Judas, would you betray me with a kiss?" Then Jesus said to the crowd of soldiers. "Have you come after me as against a robber? I was with you many days, and you did not arrest me; but this is the time for the power of darkness." Then the soldiers took Jesus, and His friends all ran away.

# Jesus is Condemned to Death

─────── ⟶ • ⟵ ───────

The soldiers took Jesus to Caiaphas, who was the high priest. Many of the scribes and the elders were assembled there also. Caiaphas asked Jesus many questions.

When morning came, the guards brought Jesus again before the elders, chief priests, and scribes. Many witnesses told false stories about Him. Jesus did not answer a word. Finally the high priest asked Him, "Are you the Messiah, the Son of God?" Jesus answered, "I am." They all cried, "He is worthy of death!" They led Jesus away to Pontius Pilate, the Roman governor. Pilate had his soldiers scourge Jesus. They hurt Him very badly. The soldiers found an old purple cloak and put it around Jesus' shoulders. They pressed a crown of thorns upon Jesus' head. The soldiers mocked Jesus, spat on Him, and struck Him, saying "Hail, King of the Jews!" Then Pilate condemned Jesus to death.

The soldiers laid a heavy cross on Jesus' shoulders and made Him carry it up to the Mount of Calvary, where He was to be crucified. Many people shouted at Jesus and made fun of Him, but others felt very sad for Jesus and were sorrowful as He staggered by under the heavy weight of the cross.

# Jesus Is Nailed to the Cross

─────── ❧ • ❧ ───────

As Jesus carried the cross on the way to Calvary, His mother Mary made her way through the crowd and came to Him. Mary felt very sad in her heart to see Jesus suffer so much, yet she knew God had allowed this, in order to save the world. She and Jesus looked at each other with great love and tears in their eyes. Then the guards pushed Jesus on His way.

When they arrived at Calvary, the soldiers took Jesus and stripped off His clothes. Then they nailed Jesus to the cross. Jesus endured all of this in silence, offering His suffering for us and for our salvation.

On top of the cross Pilate had written the letters INRI, which stood for the words, "Jesus of Nazareth, King of the Jews." The soldiers raised the cross and placed it in the ground. While Jesus hung on the cross, the chief priests and others mocked Him, saying, "He saved others; let him save himself if he is the Messiah." The soldiers also made fun of Jesus, saying, "If you are the king of the Jews, save yourself." When Jesus heard this, He still chose to love and pray for the people. Jesus prayed, "Father, forgive them, for they do not know what they do."

# Jesus Dies on the Cross

Two criminals were crucified with Jesus, one on either side of Him. One of the criminals said to Jesus, "Lord, remember me when you come into your kingdom." Jesus said to him, "This day you shall be with me in Paradise."

The soldiers took Jesus' clothes and divided them into four shares, a share for each soldier. Then they took His robe, which was woven in one piece, from top to bottom. They said, "Let us not tear this, but let us gamble to see whose it shall be." In doing this they fulfilled a prophecy regarding the Messiah:

"They divide my garments among them;
for my clothing they cast lots" (Psalm 22:18).

A great darkness covered the earth as Jesus was dying. He saw His mother Mary standing at the foot of the cross, with His beloved apostle, John. Jesus said to His mother, "Woman, behold your son." Then to John He said, "Behold your mother." From that hour John took Mary into his home. Jesus then said, "I thirst!" A soldier dipped a sponge in some common wine, and raised it to Jesus. Jesus cried out in a loud voice, "It is finished! Father, into Your hands I commit my spirit." And bowing His head, Jesus died.

# The Centurion Beholds the Son of God

--- ○●○ ---

In the Temple of God in Jerusalem there hung a beautiful purple and red curtain which separated the outer sanctuary from the inner sanctuary. When God had instructed Moses how to construct the Dwelling Place in the desert, He had commanded that this veil be hung to set apart the Holy of Holies, where the Ark of the Covenant rested. Because of the holiness of God, no one was permitted to enter the Inner Sanctuary, except the High Priest. Even he could only enter one day a year, on the Day of Atonement, to offer the blood of sacrifice on behalf of the people. When Jesus gave up His spirit in death, the curtain of the temple was torn in two, from top to bottom. God did this to show that because of Jesus' death and through the blood of His sacrifice, all people could now be reunited with God and enter heaven.

A soldier took a lance and put it into Jesus' side, and immediately there came from His heart blood and water. The earth quaked, rocks were split, and a great storm fell upon Mount Calvary. When the Roman centurion and the soldiers who had stood guard over Jesus saw the earthquake and all that was happening, they were very afraid, and exclaimed, "Truly this man was the Son of God!"

# Jesus Is Taken Down from the Cross

There were many women at Calvary, looking on from a distance. These women had followed Jesus from Galilee, ministering to Him. Among them were Mary Magdalene and Mary the mother of James and Joseph, and the mother of the sons of Zebedee.

Meanwhile, a rich man named Joseph of Arimathea, a secret disciple of Jesus, went to Pilate and asked for the body of Jesus. Pilate ordered it to be handed over. Nicodemus, another disciple of Jesus, brought oils and sweet spices to prepare Jesus' body for burial. Taking the body, they wrapped it in clean linen and sweet spices, as was the custom of the Jews. Then they laid the body of Jesus in Joseph's new tomb, which had been hewn in the rock. They rolled a huge stone across the entrance to the tomb and went home.

Mary Magdalene and the other Mary remained there, facing the tomb. The chief priests also went to Pilate, and asked him for soldiers to guard the tomb, since Jesus had said that He would rise on the third day. The priests were afraid that the disciples of Jesus would come and steal His body. Pilate gave them soldiers, who sealed the tomb and guarded it.

Margaret W. Tarrant

# Jesus Rises From the Dead!

Very early in the morning on the first day of the week, as the soldiers were guarding the tomb, the earth began to quake violently. In the middle of the earthquake, an angel of the Lord descended from heaven, approached the tomb, rolled away the stone, and sat upon it. He looked like lightning and his clothing was white as snow. The guards were so afraid that they fell down like dead men.

Just after sunrise, Mary Magdalene, Mary the mother of James, a woman named Joanna, and some other women from Galilee came to the tomb to anoint the body of Jesus. They had prepared spices and perfumed oils. As they came over the hill, they gasped in amazement. "The stone is rolled away!" they cried. They ran down to the tomb, but did not find the body of Jesus. Then they saw an angel. "Do not be afraid!" the angel said. "I know you are seeking Jesus the crucified. He is not here, for he is risen, just as he said. Come and see the place where he lay. Then go tell his disciples that he has been raised from the dead."

The women left the tomb quickly, afraid yet overjoyed, and they ran to tell the good news to the disciples.

# Peter and John Run to the Tomb

Mary Magdalene ran as fast as she could to where the apostles were staying. She went to Peter and John and cried, "They have taken the Lord from the tomb, and we don't know where they put him!" Peter and John got up immediately and ran to the tomb. John ran faster than Peter. When he arrived at the tomb he bent down and saw the burial cloths, but did not go in.

Peter arrived after John. He went into the tomb and saw the burial cloths there. He saw that the cloth that had covered Jesus' head was not with the burial cloths but was rolled up by itself in a separate place. Peter was amazed at what had happened. Then John also went in to the empty tomb. He saw and believed.

Neither Peter nor John yet understood the scripture that the Messiah had to rise from the dead. They both returned home to tell the others about the empty tomb, and the amazing things they had seen.

# Jesus Appears to Mary Magdalene

Mary Magdalene stayed outside the tomb weeping. She loved Jesus very much and had suffered greatly as she watched Him die on the cross. She wanted to believe the angel, but she did not know where Jesus was.

Mary turned around and saw a man standing near her. "Woman," He said, "why are you weeping? Whom are you looking for?" Thinking He was the gardener, Mary replied, "Sir, if you carried him away, tell me where you laid him, and I will take him." The man speaking to her was Jesus, but Mary did not recognize Him.

"Mary!" Jesus said. Mary turned to Jesus and exclaimed, "Rabbi!" Then she went to embrace Him. Jesus said to her, "Stop holding on to me, for I have not yet ascended to the Father. But go to my brothers and tell them, 'I am going to my Father and to your Father, to my God and to your God!'"

Mary was overjoyed. She left Jesus, and ran to the disciples. "I have seen the Lord!" she proclaimed. Then she told them the good news about Jesus, who had appeared to her in the garden, near the empty tomb.

# The Road to Emmaus

## ⚪ • ⚫

On the very day of the Resurrection, two disciples were
walking to a village called Emmaus, which was seven miles
from Jerusalem. While they were discussing everything that
had happened, Jesus Himself drew near and walked with
them. However, they did not recognize Him. Jesus asked them,
"What are you talking about as you walk along?" One of them
replied, "Are you the only visitor to Jerusalem who does not
know of the things that have taken place there in these days?"
"What sort of things?" Jesus asked. They replied, "The things
that happened to Jesus of Nazareth, who was a mighty prophet.
We were hoping that he would be the one to redeem Israel.
This morning, some women from our group went to the tomb
but did not find his body. They told us they had indeed seen a
vision of angels who announced that he was alive."

Jesus then shared with them the scriptures about Himself. As
they approached the village they urged Him, "Stay with us,
for it is nearly evening." While at table with them, Jesus took
bread, said the blessing, broke it, and gave it to them. With
that their eyes were opened and they recognized Him, but He
vanished from their sight. Then they said to each other, "Were
not our hearts burning within us while he spoke to us on the
way and opened the scriptures to us?"

# Jesus Ascends Into Heaven

After His resurrection, Jesus stayed on the earth for forty days, showing Himself many times to His disciples, and speaking to them about the kingdom of God. After all His life and work, after all His teaching and healing, after preparing His apostles and disciples to continue bringing the Kingdom, Jesus was now ready to leave the earth. It was time for Him to return to His Father, and to ascend into heaven.

Jesus had once told His apostles, "It is necessary that I go, in order to send to you the Comforter, the Holy Spirit, who will be with you always, until I return in glory." Now He told them, "Do not depart from Jerusalem, but wait there for 'the promise of the Father' about which I have spoken to you. John baptized with water, but in a few days you will be baptized with the Holy Spirit. You will receive power when the Holy Spirit comes upon you. Then you will be my witnesses in Jerusalem, throughout Judea and Samaria, and to the ends of the earth."

When Jesus had said this, He blessed His disciples. As they were looking on, Jesus ascended to heaven and a cloud took Him away out of their sight.

# The Holy Spirit Descends
# Upon the Apostles

After Jesus ascended into heaven, the apostles returned to Jerusalem. Mother Mary was with them, as were others who believed—about 120 persons in all. When the day of Pentecost came, they were all in one accord in the upper room of a house. Suddenly there came from heaven a noise like a strong driving wind, which filled the whole room where they were sitting. There appeared tongues as of fire, which parted and rested on each one of them, and they were all filled with the Holy Spirit. They began to speak in different tongues, as the Spirit enabled them to proclaim.

There were devout Jews from every nation staying in Jerusalem. When they heard the sound, they gathered in a large crowd around the upper room. They were confused because each one heard the apostles speaking in his own language. They asked in amazement, "Are not all these people who are speaking Galileans? Then how does each of us hear them in his own native language? We have come from all over the world, from Arabia and Asia, as well as from Rome and Greece, and Africa. Yet we hear them in our own languages praising the mighty acts of God."

# Peter Preaches at Pentecost

Peter stood up with the apostles and proclaimed to all the people, "Jesus of Nazareth was a man whom God commended to you with mighty deeds, wonders, and signs. God worked these through Jesus while he lived among you, as you yourselves know. You killed this man, using lawless men to crucify him."

Peter continued, "However, God raised Jesus. We are all witnesses. Therefore let the whole house of Israel know for certain that God has made this Jesus whom you crucified both Lord and Messiah."

When the people heard this, they felt very sad and guilty in their hearts. They asked Peter and the other apostles, "What are we to do, my brothers?" Peter said to them, "Repent and be baptized, every one of you, in the name of Jesus Christ for the forgiveness of your sins; and you will receive the gift of the Holy Spirit. For the promise is made to you and to your children and to all those far off, whomever the Lord our God will call." Peter exclaimed, "Save yourselves from this corrupt generation." Three thousand people accepted his message and were baptized that day. The Church was born!

# Peter and John Heal a Lame Man

━━━━━━━━━━━━ ❧ • ❧ ━━━━━━━━━━━━

One afternoon not long after Pentecost, Peter and John went
up to the Temple to pray. There was a man there who was lame
from birth, near a place called the Beautiful Gate. The man
could not walk. He asked Peter and John for money. "Look
at us," Peter said. The man fixed his gaze on them, hoping to
receive some coins.

Peter said, "I have neither silver nor gold, but what I do have
I give you: in the name of Jesus Christ of Nazareth, arise and
walk!" Peter took the man by his right hand and raised him up.
Immediately his feet and ankles grew strong. The man leaped
up and went into the temple with them, walking and leaping
and praising God. When all the people saw him walking
around and praising God, they recognized him as the beggar
who used to sit at the Beautiful Gate of the Temple. They were
amazed at what had happened to him. As he clung to Peter
and John, all the people hurried in toward them.

Peter then said to the people, "We did not do this by our own
power. The God of Abraham, Isaac, and Jacob has glorified
His servant Jesus. It was by faith in His name that this man has
been healed. Repent, therefore, and be converted, that your
sins may be wiped away, and that the Lord may send you the
Messiah already appointed for you, Jesus!"

# Stephen the First Martyr

The number of those who believed in Jesus continued to grow. The apostles needed helpers who could serve the people with their daily bread, so the people chose seven men to serve as deacons. The first was named Stephen. He was a man full of faith and the Holy Spirit. The word of God continued to spread with great power.

Some Jews stirred up the people and the elders against Stephen. They told lies about him, and Stephen was brought before the Sanhedrin, the place of judgement for the Jews, to be questioned. Stephen stood up and recounted the history of Israel, beginning with Abraham, Isaac, and Jacob. He spoke of how God had delivered His people from Egypt, and led them into the Promised Land.

Then Stephen said, "Why do you always oppose the Holy Spirit? You received the Law, but you did not observe it." They grew angry at him, and he said, "Behold I see the heavens opened and the Son of Man standing at the right hand of God!" Then they took him out of the city and began to stone him. They laid their cloaks at the feet of a young man named Saul. Stephen cried out, "Lord Jesus, receive my spirit! Lord, do not hold this sin against them." Then he died.

# Philip and the Ethiopian

—————— ❧ • ❧ ——————

A great persecution broke out against the church in Jerusalem. All the believers except the apostles were scattered throughout the countryside of Judea and Samaria. Philip went down to Samaria and preached about Jesus to them. God performed great signs and wonders though him. Unclean spirits came out of people and many were healed. There was great joy in that city. Then the angel of the Lord told Philip, "Get up and head down the road to Gaza."

There was an official from Ethiopia who had come to Jerusalem to worship, and was returning home. Seated in his chariot, he was reading from the book of the prophet Isaiah. The Holy Spirit told Philip, "Go and join up with that chariot." Philip ran up and heard the man reading Isaiah the prophet. He said, "Do you understand what you are reading?" The man replied, "How can I, unless someone teaches me?" He invited Philip to sit with him. Philip got in the chariot, and beginning with the passage the man was reading, he shared with him about Jesus.

They came up to some water, and the Ethiopian official asked if he could be baptized. Philip baptized him, and then the Spirit of the Lord snatched him away. The official returned home to Ethiopia, rejoicing in the Lord.

# The Conversion of Paul

Saul, who had agreed with the stoning of Stephen, entered the homes of those who believed in Jesus, dragging out men and women and handing them over for imprisonment. He then asked the high priest for letters to the synagogues in Damascus, that he might go there and bring the believers back to Jerusalem in chains.

As Saul neared Damascus, suddenly a bright light from the sky flashed around him. He fell to the ground and heard a voice saying to him, "Saul, Saul, why are you persecuting me?" Saul said, "Who are you, sir?" The reply came, "I am Jesus, whom you are persecuting. Get up and go into the city and you will be told what you must do."

The men who were with Saul heard the voice but did not see anyone. Saul got up from the ground but could see nothing, so they led him out by the hand into Damascus. For three days he neither ate nor drank. Then God told a disciple named Ananias to go to Saul. Ananias replied, "Lord, I have heard about this man, what evil things he has done to Your people." But the Lord said, "Go, for I have chosen this man to bring my name before Gentiles, kings, and Israelites." So Ananias went to Saul and laid his hands on him. Saul received his sight and was filled with the Holy Spirit. Saul then began to proclaim Jesus in the synagogues, that He is the Son of God.

# Peter's Vision of Foods Called Clean
— ෬•෧ —

In Caesarea, a city of Israel, there lived a Roman centurion named Cornelius. He loved God very much, prayed constantly, and gave offerings to the Jews for the poor. An angel appeared to him one day and said, "Your prayers and sacrifices have gone up as an offering to God. Now send some men to the city of Joppa and summon a man named Simon Peter." Cornelius immediately did as the angel said.

Meanwhile, Peter was praying on a roof in Joppa when he saw something like a large sheet come down from heaven. In it were all the four legged animals of the earth, as well as reptiles and birds. A voice said to him, "Get up Peter. Kill and eat." But Peter refused because it was against Jewish Law to eat unclean animals. The voice then said, "What God has made clean, you are not to call unclean."

The men that Cornelius had sent asked Peter to go with them, and he did. When Peter arrived, he said, "It is unlawful for a Jewish man to visit a Gentile. But God has shown me I should not call unclean what He has made clean." He then preached about Jesus to Cornelius and all his household. The Holy Spirit came upon all who heard, and they were baptized. In this way God showed that Jesus had come to bring salvation to all people, both Jews and Gentiles.

# The Gospel Spreads to the Whole World

Before Jesus ascended into heaven, He told His apostles that they would be His witnesses to the ends of the earth. After Pentecost, they spread out from Jerusalem and preached about Jesus and the good news of His salvation to the nearby areas of Phoenicia and Antioch. A disciple named Barnabas went to Antioch and encouraged the new believers there. He then left for Tarsus to look for Saul. When Barnabas found Saul, he brought him back to Antioch with him, and many people accepted the faith. It was in Antioch that the disciples were first called Christians.

However, there were difficulties as well. King Herod put the apostle James to death. He then arrested Peter, but the Lord delivered Peter from prison. After a time, Peter left Jerusalem, journeying to Antioch and eventually to Rome.

The Lord called Barnabas and Saul to the work of preaching the Gospel to the Gentiles. Barnabas and Saul, who was called Paul, set out on their first missionary journey, setting up churches throughout Asia Minor. Paul then left on a second journey, with Silas, to preach the Gospel to Greece and the surrounding regions.

# Paul Preaches the Good News

———— ☙ • ❧ ————

Paul and Silas traveled through Syria and the region of Cilicia. They encouraged the Christians there and strengthened their faith. They met a young believer named Timothy, who joined them on their mission. Day by day the churches grew stronger in faith and larger in number.

Paul and his companions set sail for Troas, and from there to Philippi, a leading city in that area. On the Sabbath they went outside the city gate along the river. There they spoke with some women about Jesus and His gift of new life. One of the women, named Lydia, listened with great interest to Paul. The Lord opened her heart to receive His word, and she and her household were baptized. She invited Paul and his friends to stay at her home. Not long afterwards, Paul and Silas were beaten and thrown into prison, but God delivered them through a great earthquake. After that, even the jailer and his family were baptized.

In city after city, Paul and the other apostles preached the word of God, and many people came to believe in Jesus and in the good news of His salvation. The believers suffered much for their faith, but they rejoiced in God who gave them His victory each and every time.

# Paul's Final Imprisonment

---

Paul traveled through Greece again, visiting all the churches. Then he traveled to Jerusalem, where some of the Jews seized Paul, dragged him out of the temple, and sought to put him to death. The Roman commander of the city rescued Paul from the crowd and then imprisoned him until he could find what he had done. Jesus appeared to Paul the following night. He stood by him and said, "Take courage. Just as you have borne witness to my cause in Jerusalem, so you must also bear witness to me in Rome."

Paul was sent to the city of Caesarea, where he was kept under house arrest for two years. Then he was sent to Rome, where he was again put under house arrest. During that time, Paul continued to preach, fearlessly proclaiming to Jews and Gentiles alike the truth about Jesus, His free gift of salvation, and the Kingdom of God.

After two years, Paul was released. He traveled to other parts of the world, and then returned to Rome where he was again imprisoned. In the year 67, the Romans beheaded Paul. Saint Paul died as a martyr for the Faith he had so valiantly lived and preached throughout the world.

# John Writes the Book of Revelation

In the last years of his life, the apostle John was banished to an island called Patmos. On Patmos, the Lord gave John an amazing set of visions. John wrote about these in the final book of the Bible, the Book of Revelation. The Book of Revelation tells of the triumph of Jesus Christ, the Lamb of God, who was slain, yet lives forever. It also tells of the many difficulties that the people of God must endure until the final triumph of the Lord.

The Book of Revelation is filled with beautiful hymns of praise, revealing the worship that is taking place already in heaven. It tells of a new Jerusalem coming down out of heaven from God. The book closes with the words, "'Surely I am coming soon.' Amen. Come Lord Jesus! The grace of the Lord Jesus be with you all."